ISBN 978-1-331-59389-8
PIBN 10210354

1 MONTH OF
FREE
READING

at

www.ForgottenBooks.com

By purchasing this book you are eligible for one month membership to ForgottenBooks.com, giving you unlimited access to our entire collection of over 700,000 titles via our web site and mobile apps.

To claim your free month visit:

www.forgottenbooks.com/free210354

English
Français
Deutsche
Italiano
Español
Português

www.forgottenbooks.com

Mythology Photography **Fiction**
Fishing Christianity **Art** Cooking
Essays Buddhism Freemasonry
Medicine **Biology** Music **Ancient
Egypt** Evolution Carpentry Physics
Dance Geology **Mathematics** Fitness
Shakespeare **Folklore** Yoga Marketing
Confidence Immortality Biographies
Poetry **Psychology** Witchcraft
Electronics Chemistry History **Law**
Accounting **Philosophy** Anthropology
Alchemy Drama Quantum Mechanics
Atheism Sexual Health **Ancient History**
Entrepreneurship Languages Sport
Paleontology Needlework Islam
Metaphysics Investment Archaeology
Parenting Statistics Criminology
Motivational

|||

CHARACTERISTICS

OF

GOETHE.

FROM THE GERMAN OF

FALK, VON MÜLLER,

&c.

WITH NOTES, ORIGINAL AND TRANSLATED,

ILLUSTRATIVE OF GERMAN LITERATURE,

BY SARAH AUSTIN.

———

IN THREE VOLUMES.

VOL. I.

LONDON:

PUBLISHED BY EFFINGHAM WILSON,

ROYAL EXCHANGE.

1833.

PREFACE.

WHEN I began this work my intention was simply to translate Falk's recollections of Goethe. It was suggested to me that many of the persons and incidents alluded to by him were little, or not at all, known to the English public, and that a few explanatory notes would not be unwelcome. The idea then presented itself that the works, or passages from works, mentioned by Falk were likewise many of them unknown here, and that I might do a still better service by appending specimens of Goethe's manifold productions, in such a form, as I could

put them into;—imperfect enough, but
still affording glimpses of some of the
varied beauties of the original. Other
valuable illustrative matter was given to
me by friends; and so, without any fore-
laid scheme, arose all this superstructure
upon Falk.

The view of Goethe's practical life then
came to hand, recommended not only by
its intrinsic value and interest, but by the
sanction and authority it had received.
Knowing, however, that the testimony
of friends and admirers neither has, nor
perhaps ought to have, much weight with
the world, and following up the thought
that Goethe must be illustrated out of
himself, I again turned to his own works,
—the record of his immediate thoughts
and feelings, and found there such cor-

roborative matter as I have annexed. I might have added ten times as much.

The Memoir by Monsieur Soret has a character and claims of its own. M. Soret's pursuits are, as we collect from himself, physical ; he is not a German ; and thus a poetical temperament and national partiality (two things which might tend to lessen the value of his testimony) are excluded. The journal from which the Memoir is extracted, though published in French, is in the hands of very few English readers.

The matter that follows requires perhaps some apology, and I was more than once tempted to exclude it, from the fear of an appearance of book-making. But I think it will be obvious that a sketch of the character and acts of Karl-August of Sachsen-Weimar can never be irrelevant or superfluous in any work of which Goethe is the subject. Independently of the interest which three persons so remarkable as the Grand Duke, his mother, and his wife, must excite, they are to be regarded as among the most important influences of Goethe's life and genius; and we may safely say that under no other ruler, or form of government, could he have been what he was. And this he clearly felt. Whether the influences were favourable, whether the effect was good, is for others to discuss. One thing, however, is to be gathered from this portion of the work, that genius, learning, and liberal thought have a far other field, and a very different hold over the hearts and minds of men

of all ranks in Germany, than here;—
that the employment of such men as
Goethe, Herder, the Humbolds, Niebuhr, Ancillon, and many others distinguished in art, philosophy, and letters,
as active functionaries of the state, is
one of the tributes which the Govern-
ments of the enlightened part of Germany pay to merit, and is completely in
harmony with the tone of public opinion.

The piece of literary criticism from the
Conversations-Lexicon seemed necessary
to complete the view of the Author and
Poet. It is brief and imperfect, but
anything like a full review of his works
was out of the question.

The extracts from the posthumous
number of *Kunst und Alterthum* afford

touching proofs of his unquenched energy, his unsubdued sympathies, and of the
devoted attachments he inspired. Here,
too, are the last lines that flowed from
that most prolific pen.

I received from Germany another little work which would have done more
to render this compilation *piquant* and
popular than anything I have inserted.
I did not, however, find it possible to
make any use of it. It is anonymous
and disparaging. (See Volume iii. p. 248.)
Now, attacks upon a great man, or sto-
ries likely to lessen him in public esti-
mation, ought at least to have the sanction of a name. We have a right to ask
upon whose authority we are called on
to give our belief to matter of so painful
a kind. And if the absence of all such

sanction determined me to reject the de-
pretiating parts of the book, I felt that
I had no right to attach any value to the
eulogies of a writer whose censures I
did not think worth notice. Nothing remained therefore but "resolutely to ig-
nore it*."

* I had the satisfaction of receiving the following
valuable corroboration of my own judgment, from a
gentleman who enjoyed the personal friendship of
Goethe, and whose name I should gladly mention if
I thought myself at liberty to do so without special
permission. The other part of his letter is too inter-
resting to be omitted.

" In compliance with your wishes, I add a few words
concerning Goethe; and particularly some remarks for
which I am indebted to a lady, a personal friend of
Goethe and his mother. She writes as follows :

" To the characteristics of Goethe's extraordinary
mother, I should add, that she had a singular art of
stimulating young and active minds, and that out of the
treasures of her own experience she instructed them in
the science of life. How did we hang on her lips when in
her joyous yet earnest manner, she related to us, then
girls of twelve or fourteen, a story by Musæus or Wieland,

Want of piety towards the specially-gifted teachers and laborious benefactors of mankind is among the commonest

or recited a poem by her son.—'She was worthy of Life!' (*Sie war des Lebens werth*) said her great son to me, in the year 1814, when he revisited his paternal city. How intense was her attachment to her friends; how efficient a mediator and helper, how faithful and discreet a confidant was she! She used to say, 'Don't lose your presence of mind because the wind blows roughly; and think on Wieland's words, *die Hand die uns durch dieses Dunkel führt* (the hand that leads us through this darkness).'

" In relation to Goethe's connection with the Grand Duke of Weimar, the poem '*Klein ist unter Germaniens, &c.*' will not escape you. [See p. 97, Vol. iii.]

" In conclusion, accept my cordial acknowledgment and approbation of your decision with regard to the calumnious '*Büchlein von Goethe.*' You judge and act according to Goethe's own maxims. 'When man,' says he at the grave of a friend, 'reflects on his physical or moral condition, he commonly discovers some hidden malady. Life, to all of us, is suffering. Who, save God alone, shall call us to our reckoning? Let no reproaches fall on the departed. Not what they have failed in, nor what they have suffered, but what they have *done*, what they have accomplished, ought to occupy the survivors.

and yet the most lamentable proofs of barren imagination and defective morality.

> " Es liebt die Welt das Glänzende zu schwarzen
> Und das Erhabene in dem Staub zu ziehen."

But we need no ' revelations ' to teach us this melancholy and humiliating truth —that " by his failings we know him to be Man,"—one of ourselves,—tainted with the faults with which we all abound. It is no time for flippant exultation when we see that the brightness of the most

By the failings we recognize the species ; by the excellencies, the individual. Defects we have all in common ;—virtues belong to each severally.'

" The common people in Weimar called Goethe, ' our old, kind gentleman,' (*unser alter guter Herr*). When he was here he visited all the friends of his youth who were still living. He also sought out every individual who had paid his mother attention, and thanked them all."

Frankfurt on Main, Dec. 22d, 1833.   E. L. H.

glorious specimens of our race is spotted and bedimmed in a thousand ways. It were more profitable to ask wherein they excelled us, and how they reached that excellence.

It was suggested to me by an accomplished German scholar by whose opinion I am generally glad to be guided, that I should do better to work up all these separate materials into a regular biographical work. I ventured to think otherwise. It seems to me that the incompleteness, the repetitions, and the disjointedness of this work are more than atoned for by the perfect authenticity and individuality of each portion. Each bears the name and the character of some competent and trustworthy witness. Above all, I preferred this plan,

inasmuch as it reduced my own share in
the work to what might easily be rejected without prejudice to the substan-
tive matter. Insignificant as it is, I
sincerely wish it less. My anxiety to
convey the exact meaning of the original
and the frequent impossibility of finding
adequate words, has betrayed me into
explanations which, I am sensible, may
be thought tedious and pedantic.

I have also been told that I should
be expected to offer some opinion on
Goethe's character and works. To this
I feel myself thoroughly incompetent.
I envy, but am unable to imitate, the
facility with which many writers of the
day, even in this country, have made up
their minds as to the character, opinions,
and writings of this extraordinary man.

What I could offer would be but conjecture, and if at any time I think I see more clearly, it is probably only where none can mistake.

I should be glad to refer unconditionally to the writings of my friend Mr. Carlyle, to whom respect and admiration would always incline me to defer, and whose views of Goethe I wish to share, but I confess that he has arrived at more confident conclusions than I can come to ;—probably because he sees further. If I were to venture on any observations, it would be rather with the view of suggesting some of the obstacles that seem to exist in peculiar force in this country to the understanding of Goethe, than with the remotest idea of guiding the judgments of others.

The materials now submitted to the English reader suffice to show that quality which struck all who approached his person, and must strike all who study his works; his universality. By this it is not meant that he acquired or produced a number of things; that distinction he would share with many—with Voltaire for instance; yet no man is less entitled to the praise of many-sidedness than Voltaire; for whether in prose or verse, history or fiction, we are certain of meeting the same trains of associations, opinions, and prejudices throughout his works.

But Goethe had the singular faculty of divesting himself of intellectual identity—of becoming that which he contemplated or described—of feeling the sensations, of thinking the thoughts, of other beings. To be able to follow him in his infinitely excursive travels into every region of the Actual and the Possible—to consider all the questions that most interest and agitate mankind with perfect *indifferency* (using the word in Locke's sense)—requires an imagination as mobile, a temper as impartial, an understanding as large as his. Where are they to be found? To most men (particularly in a country where the divisions of class and sect are so strongly marked as in England) it would be just as possible to transform themselves bodily into the outward form of another. To them every writer necessarily appears intent on attacking or defending, openly or covertly, the opinions, actions, or characters of some party. But, it cannot be too often repeated, Goethe was *not* a partisan. He observed and described. And his power of identifying himself with every state or mode of human existence was not at all confined to those aspects it has already exhibited. His imagination could present him with new situations, new influences, and new results, with equal truth and vivacity. Of this I might suggest many examples.

It is a total mistake to confound these speculations on possible changes in the forms of society, with arguments in their favour.

That he was indifferent to the progress of human improvement, and the sum of human happiness, as some have affirmed, appears to me incredible. It is difficult to conceive what motive could have induced a man laden with years and honours, and secure in affluence, to persevere in labours like his to the last hour of life. Indifferent to many of the questions that are most fiercely debated, he might,—nay rather he *must*—be, for his wide and prophetic glance pierced far beyond the strife of the hour. To those who required of him to join in it, he might well reply,

" Mortale est quod quæris opus ; mihi fama perennis
   Quæritur :"—

and not only perennial fame, but, as its inseparable concomitant, perennial usefulness—usefulness which will be recognized by grateful generations long after the waves which today agitate the ocean of life shall have subsided and given place to others;—or, if that may ever be, to calm. Maxims of the most profound, earnest, and enlarged humanity; benign indulgence for frailty; schemes and hopes of improvement; exhortations to labour for the good of mankind, are thickly scattered through his works: are we then justified in accusing him of apathy and selfishness because he had a dread of violent political convulsions; a distrust of the efficacy of abrupt changes in the mechanism of government?

It was not, surely, that he was indifferent to the welfare of mankind, but that he thought it a pernicious illusion to look for healing to sources whence he was persuaded healing could never come. His labours for the improvement of the human race were unwearied, calm, and systematic. But if the political neutrality he obstinately observed subjected him to the vehement denunciations of many of his countrymen, it will probably be still more revolting to English readers. It is, however, unreasonable to expect the same earnestness and vehemence in support of any cause or system from a man who sees it with all its limitations and possible attendant evils, as from one who can perceive nothing but its advantages. The same clear, serene, far-reaching glance which enabled him to discern "the soul of goodness in things evil," and thence inclined him to tolerance and indulgence, revealed to him the evil that lurks amid the greatest apparent good, and thus moderated his expectations and tempered his zeal.

Another obstacle to the understanding of Goethe's views and works presents itself in remarkable force in this country. I mean the notions of Art which prevail here, and the absence of æsthetical education.

Goethe was called, preeminently, *the Artist.* It was the title in which he delighted, and of which he was proud; and justly. But we must remember that he regarded Art not as the minister to the senses, or the imagination, or the fancy; not, on the other hand, as the mere mask or gilding wherewith to cover the awful and repulsive countenance of morals or of science, and accommodate them to human weakness and indolence; but as essentially, and in and for itself, moral, humanizing, beneficent—the expositor of the Beautiful and the Good. In his view of the matter, therefore, there could be no more vulgar mistake than that confusion of the province of ethics and æsthetics which reigns here.

On the one hand, there has sprung up an impatience of all purely didactic works. It seems to be generally admitted that nobody now reads the great teachers of philosophy or morals. On the other, as people are unwilling to relinquish the appearance of learning, they require of writers of fiction to weave into their works such shreds of information as may suffice to keep up the agreeable illusion of the acquisition of knowledge. Children are trained in this confusion of ideas. Labour, the high duty and condition of life, and Art, its purifier, consoler, and charm, are both debased; the one is regarded as an enemy to be eluded; the other, as useless, trifling, if not pernicious, in itself, but conveniently lending itself to the cheat. It is true that a work of Art may be made to inculcate *a moral* (as it is vulgarly called), or to teach a scientific truth—just as the Apollo Belvedere might serve as a tailor's block—but are these the aims of Art?

I am aware that nothing can be more unfashionable than this view of the subject, or than the doubt whether anything great, either didactic or æsthetic, will be produced under this system. If it be said that this view of Art implies indifference to the moral tone and tendency of a work, it can only be replied, that such an objection implies a belief that moral truth and beauty may be violated without injury to æsthetical perfection ;—a mistake into which no true Artist could fall.

But I have ventured much further than I intended. I affect not to explain *any-thing* in Goethe ;—only to suggest the chief causes which, as it seems to me, render him difficult to understand in all countries, and more peculiarly in this*. The truth is, I have never yet met with a German who affected to understand Goethe throughout. How far this is his

---

* What has been said relates to his works—the deliberate expressions of his opinions. There are parts of his conversations with Falk which, I confess, appear to me mere effusions of a wanton fancy, to which its possessor gave the reins in the freedom of private intercourse.

fault I do not take upon me to discuss, much less to decide. It is possible that "the Mysterious, the Sibylline, the Iucoherent," in his writings has no meaning —but it seems unlikely.

"Whatever I comprehend," says Mr. Coleridge, speaking of Plato's Timæus, "impresses me with a reverential sense of the author's genius; but there is a considerable portion of the work, to which I can attach no consistent meaning. In other treatises of the same philosopher intended for the average comprehensions of men, I have been delighted with the masterly good sense, with the perspicuity of the language, and the aptness of the inductions. I recollect likewise, that numerous passages in this author, which I thoroughly comprehend,

were formerly no less unintelligible to
me than the passages now in question.
It would, I am aware, be quite *fashionable* to dismiss them at once as Platonic
Jargon. But this I cannot do with satisfaction to my own mind, because I have
sought in vain for causes adequate to the
solution of the assumed inconsistency. I
have no insight into the possibility of a
man so eminently wise, using words with
such half-meanings to himself, as must
perforce pass into no-meaning to his
readers. When, in addition to the mo-
tives thus suggested by my own reason,
I bring into distinct remembrance the
number and the series of great men,
who, after long and zealous study of
these works, had joined in honouring
the name of PLATO with epithets that
almost transcend humanity, I feel that a

contemptuous verdict on my part might argue want of modesty, but would hardly be received by the judicious as evidence of superior penetration. Therefore, utterly baffled in all my attempts to understand the ignorance of Plato, I CONCLUDE MYSELF IGNORANT OF HIS UNDERSTANDING*."

Long as this preface is, I would fain add a few words on the only matter connected with this book in which I have a personal interest—the theory of translation. "When languages are formed upon different principles," says **Dr. Johnson,** "it is impossible that the same modes of expression should always be elegant in both. While they run on together, the closest translation may be considered as

* Biographia Literaria, p. 237.

the best; but when they divaricate, each must take its natural course. Where correspondence cannot be obtained, it is necessary to be content with something equivalent. ' Translation, therefore,' says Dryden, ' is not so loose as paraphrase, nor so close as metaphrase*'."

* " A translation," says Novalis, "is either grammatical, or paraphrastic (*verändernd*, altering), or mythic. Mythical translations are translations in the highest style. They present the pure, essential, perfect character of the individual work of art. They do not give us the actual work, but its Ideal. As yet there exists, I believe, no complete model in this kind. It requires a head thoroughly imbued with both the poetical and the philosophical spirit, in their entire plenitude. The Greek mythology is, in part, a mythical translation of a national religion.

" Grammatical translations are translations in the ordinary sense of the word. They demand great learning, but only discursive faculties.

" Paraphrastic translations, to be genuine, require the highest poetical spirit. They easily degenerate into travesties, like Pope's Homer, &c. The true translator in this kind must, indeed, be himself the Artist, and be

"All polished languages have different styles; the concise, the diffuse, the lofty, and the humble. In the proper choice of style consists the resemblance which Dryden exacts from the translator. He is to exhibit his author's thoughts, in such a dress of diction as the author would have given them had his language been English: rugged magnificence is not to be softened; hyperbolical ostentation is not to be repressed; nor sententious affectation to have its point blunted. A translator is to be like his author; it is not his business to excel

able to give the Idea of the Whole, thus or thus, at his pleasure. He must be the poet of the poet, and thus be able to make him speak at once after his own original conception, and after that which exists in his (the translator's) mind.

"Not books alone, every thing, may be translated in these three modes."

him. The reasonableness of these rules seems sufficient for their vindication."— *(Life of Dryden).*

Now this is true as far as it goes ; but the view taken by Dryden and Johnson seems to me onesided. For it may be that the very thing I want to know is, what *are* the " modes of expression " which are, or were, esteemed elegant in another language. Here is an important key to all that constitutes the individual character of the poetry of a nation, nay of the nation itself ;—a key which, according to Dr. Johnson, the translator is to hide or to falsify.

It appears to me that Goethe alone (so far as I have seen) has solved the problem. In his usual manner he turned the subject on all sides, and saw that there are two aims of translation, perfectly distinct, nay opposed; and that the merit of a work of this kind is to be judged of entirely with reference to its aim.

" There are two maxims of translation;" says he, " the one requires that the author of a foreign nation be brought to us in such a manner that we may regard him as our own; the other, on the contrary, demands of us that we transport ourselves over to him, and adopt his situation, his mode of speaking, his peculiarities. The advantages of both are sufficiently known to all instructed persons, from masterly examples*."

* The last number of *Kunst und Alterthum* contains an article on the history of translation by Professor Riemer.

Here then " the battle between free and literal translation," as the accomplished writer of an article in the last Edinburgh Review calls it, is set at rest for ever, by simply showing that there is nothing to fight about; that each is good with relation to its end—the one, when matter alone is to be transferred, the other, when matter and form. Where the form and colour of an author is important, a translation which so far obliterates them as to "substitute the dress of diction the author would have used had his language been English," is, to my way of thinking, a failure. And for this reason I never could prevail on myself to read Pope's Homer. Before I have read ten lines I feel that it is a cheat, and I find it impossible to take the least interest in a work in which the

the very peculiarities I want to know are effaced, and replaced by others. The truth is, that I want to know not only *what*, but *how* Homer wrote. A nation that demands of its translators that they give its own *tournure* to all works of foreign growth, will have bad translations—flat, colourless, or repulsively incongruous.

The praise, that a translated work might be taken for an original, is acceptable to the translator only when the original is a work in which *form* is unimportant. A light narrative, a scientific exposition, or a plain statement of facts, which pretends to nothing as a work of art, cannot be too thoroughly naturalized. Whatever may be thought of the difficulties in the way of this kind of translation, they are slight compared with those attending the other kind, as any body who carefully studies the master-pieces in this way must perceive. In the former kind the requisites are two—the meaning of the author, and a good vernacular style: in the latter, the translator has, as far as possible, to combine with these the idiomatic tone of the author—to place him before the reader with his national and individual peculiarities of thought and of speech. The more rich, new, and striking these peculiarities are, the more arduous will the task become; for there is manifestly a boundary line, difficult if not impossible to define, beyond which the most courageously faithful translator dares not venture, under pain of becoming unreadable. This must be mainly determined by the plasticity of his language and by the taste of his fellow-countrymen. A German translator can effect, and may venture, more than an English; an English, than a French;—and this, not only because his language is more full and pliant, but because Germans have less nationality, and can endure unusual forms of speech for the sake of gaining accurate insight into the characteristics of the literature of other countries.

I shall be told that this is a mere *plaidoyer* in favour of the Germanisms with which I have made bold to affright English readers. I confess it. I do not wish to be thought unconscious of them, still less so presumptuously careless as to suffer them to stand without apology.

I should feel even more diffident than I do in submitting to the public so defective and ill-constructed a book, if I were not encouraged by the profound interest the subject is calculated to inspire, the slender means English readers as yet possess of appretiating him, and the intrinsic beauty and value of the passages which serve as illustrations.

The most remarkable works published in Germany concerning Goethe, of which I have any knowledge, are

1. " *Ueber Goethe. Literarische und artistische Nachrichten herausgegeben von Alfred Nicolovius.*" Leipsig, 1828. A collection of fragments, containing the opinions of all his cotemporaries concerning the man and his works; lists of the

pictures, prints, busts, and medals of him, and a catalogue of all the editions of his works :—rather a curious book of reference than a book to read. The editor or compiler is Goethe's grand-nephew. (See Vol. iii. p. 105.)

2. " *Goethe in den Zeugnissen der Mit-lebenden.*"—Berlin, 1823. By Varnhagen von Ense: which I have not been so for-tunate as to see. It is, like the fore-mentioned, a collection of opinions on Goethe, but I hear is a more interesting work. Of considerable volumes written specially on Goethe I know only these two; there are very likely more, but the whole literature of Germany for the last half century is full of him, and I do not remember to have looked into any im-portant work in which he is not men-

tioned or alluded to, or in which the impulse given by him to the national mind is not evident. One of the most remarkable proofs of this is afforded by a passage in the last volume of Niebuhr's Roman History. We see the immense value that illustrious and virtuous man, whose strongest passion was the love of truth, set upon Goethe's approbation. Yet their characters were as different as their pursuits. Though the Foreign Quarterly Review has noticed this, I cannot forbear quoting it.

" Our fathers, ere we, who are now old, were born, recognized in Götz and the other poems of a young man who was of the same age as Valerius in his first consulship (twenty-three), the poet who towers far above all whom our nation numbers, and who never can be excelled. Goethe has enjoyed this recognition for more than half a century; already the third generation of grown men looks up to him as the first man of the nation, without a second, and without a rival; and children hear his name, as formerly among the Greeks they did that of Homer. He has lived to see our literature, mainly on his own account, acknowledged and honoured by foreigners; but he has outlived in it the age of poetry and of youth, and has remained solitary and alone. May he, nevertheless, rejoicing in his everlasting strength, long abide cheerfully amongst us, receiving from us as old men the homage which, as boys, we rendered him! May I be enabled to offer him this history complete, on which he has bestowed his favour!"

In time, probably, a qualified biographer of Goethe will arise. Meanwhile, as M. Soret says, "his life is in his works;" and it is only to those who are prevented from studying it there, that this humble attempt to make known some few of his " characteristics " is offered.

S. A.

London, May 23d, 1833.

Joh. Dan. Falk, *Legationsrath* (Counsellor of Legation) in the Grand Duchy of Weimar, was born at Danzig in 1770. His early love of learning had to contend with great difficulties. His father, a poor wig-maker, had scarcely been able to afford him scanty instruction in reading and writing, when he required his assistance in his business, and tried by every means to stifle the boy's desire for knowledge. Resistance, however, did but increase it, and he expended all his small pittance of savings in hiring books. He read day and night the works of Gellert, Wieland, Lessing, &c. as he could find opportunity. Often, in the winter's nights of that severe climate, he used to stand and read under a lamp in the open street. His discontent with his situation grew with his years. He determined to leave his father's house, and to go to sea. He accordingly ran away, and wandered about for several days in the forests on the coast; but as the masters of vessels refused to take him on board, because he could not speak English, he was obliged to return. At length he obtained his father's leave to enter on a regular course of study. At sixteen he entered the gymnasium, where he had the advantage of excellent instruction, but had still to struggle with want. After attending the gymnasium of Danzig for six years, he went to Halle, where he studied under Wolf, Forster, Klein, &c. In 1793 he left Halle, and repaired to Weimar, where he rendered himself independent by his industry and acquirements. In 1806, when the French marched through Weimar, and in the eventful time which succeeded the battle of Jena, he had an opportunity of rendering important service to the town of Weimar, which the Duke rewarded by appointing him *Legationsrath*, with a salary. Still greater were the services Falk rendered to the suffering and the helpless. In 1813, when Saxony was invested by friends and foes, the misery of the deserted children, and the corruption which might be expected to be the consequence, oppressed his heart, softened by the loss of four promising children, who died in one month, of typhus. He laid the foundation of an association which is still most beneficent. Its prime object was to provide forsaken children, who had been suffered to run wild, with instruction in useful trades. Up to the year 1824 Falk had sent out above two hundred and fifty apprentices (*Lehrbursche*), as journeymen (*Gesellen*); Some of the boys studied at the university, others became schoolmasters, merchants, artists; most of the girls went into service. This institution gave birth to similar ones at Jena, Erfurt, Berlin, &c. As writer, he first appeared in satire, and was so favourably noticed by Wieland, that the highest expectations were excited. Indeed, his first satires, *Die Gräber von Rom*, and *Die Gebete*, were full of wit. In 1823, after other works, appeared his dramatic poem *Prometheus*, an admirable and profound work, but deficient in harmony and perfection of detail. He published novels and tales, a journal, and the *Classical Theatre of England and France*. In 1817 he commemorated the third jubilee of the Reformation, by two beautiful poems, in stanzas—*Johannes Falk's Liebe, Leben, und Leiden in Gott*. He died on the 14th February, 1826. The institution he had founded has been supported by friends, aided by the government.—*Conversations-Lexicon*.

lity. Many who knew his father intimately declare that his son's gait, and the position of his hands, were precisely his.

His mother was of a cheerful temper and quick joyous senses, such as are frequently born amid the vineyards and sunny hills of the Rhine; and as she was considerably less advanced in years than her husband, she took every thing more lightly and pleasantly than he did. She sometimes said, in her sportive way, alluding to her having been married so young, and a mother at sixteen or seventeen, " My Wolfgang and I have always gone on very well together : the reason is, we are both young, and not so far asunder in age as Wolfgang and his father."

Many a wild frolic of her son's which his austere father would hardly have passed over, she regarded with true motherly loving indulgence, or, rather, heartily entered into.

Once, for instance, at a skating party, when she and a female friend were sitting in a sledge, looking at this animating sport of youth, Wolfgang took off her cloak, hung it around him, and darted to and fro on the ice for some time before he brought it back to her. She laughed gaily, and told him it was very becoming to him.

At a later period when, in conformity with his father's advice, Goethe commenced his civil life, and submitted to the drudgery of an attorney's office, his mother veiled many things with the mantle of love, which his father would have found it difficult to forgive. In the same degree in which the somewhat stern father tried to keep his eyes open to Wolfgang's neglect of his profession, did the indulgent mother seek to close them. Many a manuscript of the youthful author* was suddenly transformed

---

* Goethe was only nineteen when he wrote the " Mitschuldiger."

into a pretended deed: many a little invitation to an innocent garden pic-nic, with young gay companions, into a note from some client.

The amiable Corona Schroeter (3), for whom Goethe afterwards wrote his " Iphigenie," at Weimar, used to tell many anecdotes of this kind in the most delightful manner. Much, indeed, of what relates to Goethe's early life, in the subsequent part of this work, I carefully wrote down in my journal from her mouth.

At an advanced period of her life, when she had been tormenting herself for weeks together, and making bitter complaints of the infirmities of age, Goethe's mother said to a friend who called on her, and asked her how she was, " Thank God, I am once more contented with myself, and can endure myself now for a few weeks to come. Lately I have been quite intolerable, and have turned against God Almighty like a little child who knows not what he would have.

" Yesterday, however, I could not bear myself any longer, and so I scolded myself heartily, and said, ' Shame on thee, old *Räthin* (Counselloress), thou hast had happy days enough in the world, and thy Wolfgang to boot; and now, when the evil days come, thou must e'en take it kindly, and not make these wry faces. What dost thou mean by being so impatient and naughty when it pleases God to lay thy cross upon thee? What then, thou wantest to walk on roses for ever? now, when thou art past the time too—past seventy!' Thus, you see, I talked to myself, and directly after my heart was lighter and all went better, because I myself was not so naughty and disagreeable."

Those who were at all acquainted with Goethe's person and manners will instantly agree with me, that much of this amiable temper, and of this vein of *naïf* humour, which nothing in life or death could subdue, flowed in full tide from her veins into his. We shall give further proofs of this hereafter, from the history of his earlier years ; as well as of his more serious moods, from the later.

CHAPTER II.

Goethe's manysidedness.—His turn for observation.— " Metamorphosis of Plants."—" Doctrine of Colours." —Biographies of Wieland and Johann Heinrich Voss.— Goethe a calm observer of events.—Incompatibility of this character with that of a partisan.—The bent of his mind opposed to that of the public mind of his time.—Unjust charges brought against him.—Defence.—Goethe's opinion of Meyer.—His value for experience as opposed to hypothesis.—His love of the natural as distinguished from the acquired or the artificial.—His candour.

GOETHE'S manysidedness*, both in art, and in the accurate perception of character, and of external objects generally, has been much celebrated, even by those who

* After the word *vielseitigkeit,* the author inserts, between brackets, *objectivität.* Those who are at all familiar with German literature, or with the language of the Kantian philosophy, which has insinuated itself into that literature to a degree perhaps to be regretted, will understand that *objectivity* means power or habit

hunt after the universal diffusion of knowledge, now so much in vogue, with the voracity of an empty stomach.

It is doubtless an entirely peculiar privilege of his genius, that he had the power of absolutely and sensibly losing himself in the object, whatever it was, to which, at any particular point of time, his attention was directed; whether it were man, beast, bird, or plant: nay, that he, to a certain extent, transformed himself in imagination into the very thing itself.

It cannot be denied that Goethe's greatness, as observer of nature and as poet; his style, his mode of thinking, his power of depicting objects, his originality; I might almost say the whole weakness, as well as the whole strength, of his moral and intel-

of employing the senses and intellect on external objects. It is opposed to *subjectivity, i. e.* power or habit of employing the mind on its own internal operations—on itself.—*Transl.*

lectual being, must be sought in this objective turn of mind.

How often have I heard him, when he
wanted to give himself up to an investigation of this kind, earnestly entreat his
friends not to disturb him with the thoughts
of others upon the subject; alledging that
it was a rigid invariable maxim with him,
when in such moods, to keep aloof all
external influences. It was not till he had
exhausted his own powers on the matter;
had, as it were, confronted it, and spoken
with it alone, that he would go into the representations or views of others: then, it
delighted him to know what others, long
before him, had thought, done, or written,
on the same subject. He then, with great
honesty and candour, corrected his mis-
takes in this or that particular; while, on
the other hand, he was filled with a child-
like delight, when he saw that, by his unaided, original efforts, he had gained here

and there a new view of the phenomenon.

How many things did nature thus reveal
to her darling, in the silent, solitary path of
mental enquiry and inward debate, which
so few are capable of treading! And, as
old fables tell us that plants, stones, flowers,
clouds, and light, have all their several voice
and utterance, so it cannot be denied that
our old German Magus (to continue the
figure) was deeply versed in the language
of birds and flowers, and was able to inter-
pret it to others.

His "Metamorphosis of Plants" (4), (*Metamorphose der Pflanzen*), his " Doctrine
of Colours," (*Farbenlehre*), are beautiful
monuments of his calm spirit of investigation: they are, so to speak, filled with the inspired glimpses of the seer, reaching deep
into distant ages, and into the hidden domain of science ; while, on the other hand,
his biographical delineations of two cha-

racters so utterly different from his own as those of Wieland and Johann Heinrich Voss (5), sufficiently manifest, not so much his literary skill, as his own beautiful nature, which could take in every object in all its genuineness and purity, and reflect it back like a clear, spotless mirror. Wieland's biography becomes the living Wieland; and Johann Heinrich Voss appears, in Goethe's delineation, stripped of all the angularities and callouses which render the course. of life so difficult. It is as if Goethe were this very Johann Heinrich Voss himself; so admirably does the great Master know how to bring before our eyes the education of this learned and singular man (wrung with toil and difficulty from untoward external circumstances), to its full completion; and to make it intelligible to us with all its details and peculiarities.

As this lofty talent of Goethe has been universally acknowledged, so, on the other hand, has he been as loudly reproached with the luke-warmness of his moral sentiments, as far as these can be inferred from his writings. His admirers at first sought to destroy the force of this censure, by alledging that the proper province of art is to withdraw itself wholly from moral considerations, and from all the rigorous restraints they impose. As a consequence of this assumption, all those who expressed their dissatisfaction at certain over-free delineations of Goethe's muse, were pronounced, without further ceremony, narrow-minded bigots. From this time it seemed as if a loose was given to a multitude of licentious productions, in which all that was highest and holiest was too often made the sport of the lowest human passion; nay, even the cloak of the coarsest sensuality.

It appears to me that the disputants on both sides overlooked a main point throughout the whole discussion. A mind like that of Goethe, in which a calm observation of all things was an innate and characteristic quality, could by no possibility fall into that moral enthusiasm which the age exacted, and which it was too much inclined to consider as the highest possible prerogative of human nature. Goethe was born to identify himself with things; not things with himself. From the moment in which the public enters the lists with passion against real or supposed evil, it cares little to examine the good sides which this very evil, if considered with perfect calmness, might perhaps present to the eye of the observer.

Thus was Goethe placed, even by the highest and noblest peculiarity of his nature, in direct opposition with his age. Goethe wanted to observe—his age wanted to act; and to seize upon every occasion, however slight, which presented itself as a possible reason for action. It was this which once led him to say to me, "Religion and politics are a troubled element for Art; I have always kept myself aloof from them as much as possible." There was but one party for which, with such views, he could declare himself: that, namely, under whose influence tranquillity might be expected, or even hoped for, let it be found how it might.

But it happened that religion and politics, church and state, were exactly the cardinal points within which the age in which he lived was destined to be remodelled. All science, and all action, were irresistibly determined by the spirit of the age to this centre. A way was forced through the most intricate questions; and the Many, with their dark and confused notions of their own condition and interests, shared the universal tendency, without any distinct conception of what was passing, or of its operation on themselves.

of the soul which animates Goethe's works, or acquire the least right to form a judgement of our own on so extraordinary and unique a man.

Goethe, too, plied his wings, and was as industrious as a bee; but his activity was the pure activity of the artist*; consequently of a totally different kind from the bustling activity of the man who struggles in and with the world. The domain of Science, such as it had been extending itself through ages; the kingdoms of Nature and of Art, whether in their earliest rise or their gradual developement;—these were the regions which he traversed with unwearied wing; and whatever treasures he collected during his long excursive flights, were

---

* I do not think it necessary to deprive myself of the use of this high and comprehensive epithet, because it happens to have been vulgarised and restricted in England, or made ridiculous in France. English readers must try to understand it in the large and refined sense in which alone it can apply to Goethe.—*Transl.*

brought home and shared with the friends whom he thus enriched and delighted.

For his own part, he thought it better to spare mankind, already sufficiently vexed and worried on all sides, all more remote and abstract questions; nor when he excited their sympathy in any of his enquiries, or afforded them instruction and delight, did he ask for any other proof of gratitude from them, than that they would abstain from roughly touching him and such kindred spirits as were given to speculations like his own, with the iron arm of reality; or from startling them out of the beautiful dreams of past ages, in which they love to indulge, into the Present.

But if this happened, the pleasant roughness of the gipsey chief, in the "Fair at Plundersweilern," (*Jahrmarkt zu Plundersweilern*) was heard again from his mouth.

Lumpen und Quark
Der ganze Markt! &c.

This theme, only a little changed, as in that hymn,

" Ich hab' mein Sach auf Nichts gestellt," &c. (6).

which is in truth only a variation of the former, was a pervading one with Goethe, and formed, so to speak, a part of his peculiar view of life.

Utterly unjust, I may say, enviously calumnious, is the charge brought against him, that he was false to his own genius, and devoted it, with interested and servile views, to the spirit of the circumstances and times in which he lived. No one ever, in all his works, through all the maxims he laid down, through all the impulses which proceeded from him, so uniformly and deliberately attended solely to his permanent and cosmopolitan fame and importance. It is true that both the church and the state will hereafter have cause to rejoice in the fruits of this majestic tree of true German race and growth; though, strangely enough, every consideration relating to church or state was carefully excluded from his mind during the formation of his own opinions and taste. We may therefore truly assert that, for any influence which Goethe will exercise in future on these subjects, we have to thank nature alone; since, as I have already observed, whatever he did was utterly without view to that end. But, as he resigned the Present almost with indifference, and freed himself from all passion in the contemplation of it, so much the nearer did he draw to the Future. In all that regards science and art, that Future will assuredly give ear to him, and will hail him as one of her most unsuspected witnesses; nay, truest harbingers. Indications, and data enough, for untwisting the tangled sk in of the Present lie scattered throughout his works. Posterity will collect them.

I by no means impute this propensity to

him as any remarkable merit, as I have already said; I only wish to adduce it as a quite peculiar prerogative of his clear nature, in which all the gifts of intuition* were concentrated, as in a crystal lens; the more, because this view of the subject is the only one which can adequately protect him against the often unmerited reproaches of the better and nobler of his friends, or of those who required at his hands things which would have placed him in utter contradiction with the most beautiful part of his own character.

They did not reflect that it was as absurd to expect of the author of "Goetz of Berlichingen" that he should throw his iron hand into the political scale against the magistrate and his despicable helper's-helper in

---

* *Alle Gaben der Beschaulichkeit.* It might be Englished, *all the perceptive faculties,* with some approach to the meaning, but with no adequate expression of it. *Beschauen* is more than to perceive, for it is to look at attentively, to examine and seek into—*intueor.*—*Transl.*

the town-hall of Heilbronn, with crushing weight and pressure (7), as to require that the sturdy Goetz himself should write, with that same iron hand of his, a pleasant masque, or an " Iphigenie," or a " Tasso." If, on the contrary, we are content to demand of Goetz what appertains to Goetz, and of Goethe what appertains to Goethe (as, in compliance with nature, we unquestionably ought), the right position for judging of both will be found.

An expression which Goethe once used with regard to our noble-minded friend Meyer (8), the painter and critic, has always struck me as remarkable, and might perhaps be applied with greater justice to himself. " All of us," said he, " without exception,—Wieland, Herder, Schiller,—have suffered ourselves to be duped by the world on one point or another ; and for that very reason, if we could return to it hereafter, it would, at least, not give us a bad reception.

"But in Meyer, long as I have known him, I never could discover anything of the kind. He is so clear-headed, and on all points, on all occasions, has so calm and perfect an apprehension; he sees what he sees so through and through, so without all mixture of passion, or of the troubled spirit of party, that the reverse of the cards which nature plays with us here below cannot possibly be hidden from him. But for that very reason the return of his spirit to this scene is out of the question; for nature does not like that we should look, uninvited, so far into her game; and when from time to time a man arises who catches one of her secrets, ten others immediately start up, who industriously conceal it again."

Goethe, by his very nature, cannot, must not, will not, set a single step which may compel him to quit the territory of experience, on which he has so firmly and so happily planted his foot, and taken root for more than half a century.

All conclusions, observations, doctrines, opinions, articles of faith, have value in his eyes only in so far as they connect themselves with this territory, which he has so fortunately conquered. The blue horizon beyond it, which man is wont to paint to himself in such beautiful colours, troubled him little; indeed he shunned it, knowing, as he did, that it is the abode of all brain-woven fantasies, and that all the phantoms of dim and gloomy superstition (which he hated) held their throne there.

He listened with patient, nay grateful, attention to all attempts to substantiate the Possible, whether good or bad, such as it presents itself in all directions within the limits of experience.

Even virtue, laboriously and painfully acquired, was distasteful to him. I might almost affirm, that a faulty but vigorous character, if it had any real native qualities as its basis, was regarded by him with more indulgence and respect than one which at no moment of its existence is genuine; which is incessantly under the most unamiable constraint, and cousequently imposes a painful constraint on others. "Oh," said he, sighing, on such occasions, "if they had but the heart to commit some absurdity! That would be something,—and they would at least be restored to their own natural soil, free from all hypocrisy and acting. Wherever that is the case, one may entertain the cheering hope that something will spring from the germ of good which nature implants in every individual; but on the ground they are now upon, nothing can grow."

"Pretty dolls!" was his common expression, when speaking of them. Another favourite phrase was, "That's a piece of nature* ;" which from Goethe's lips was considerable praise.

With questions concerning time, space, mind, matter, God, immortality, and the like, Goethe occupied himself little. Not that he denied the existence of beings superior to ourselves. By no means: they were foreign to his pursuits, only because they lay completely out of the region of experience, to which, upon system, he exclusively devoted himself. Repugnance to the super-sensual † was an inherent part of his mind ; and which among us is bold enough to engage in a boundary dispute with Nature? Had Goethe been a Leibnitz or a Kant, we should have had, instead of an " Iphigenie" and a " Faust," an

---

* *Das ist eine Natur*--literally, that is a Nature.-- *Transl.*

† *Uber-sinnlich.* I take the liberty to translate into Latinized English a word, of which we are much in want: *superhuman* and *supernatural* both miss the mark.-- *Transl.*

able system of Metaphysic ; but as he was Goethe, it is but fair to allow him to be and to remain Goethe, at all points, and in all respects.

As he once beautifully remarked in conversation with me, "In the series of the manifold productions whereby the creative powers of Nature became visible, man was, so to speak, the first dialogue that she held with God." And thus might one say of himself, that he, by his stubborn persistency within the limits of experience, represented the last product of plastic Nature ; revealing, together with her secrets, the two tendencies which lay hidden in her from eternity, and which, spite of all apparent contradictions, must be taken together to form a true, entire, and perfect creation ; a view of things which might afford no contemptible addition to the definition of what we call genius. For as genius, from the moment in which it breaks away from nature, wanders into the most unpleasant labyrinths and not unfrequently falls into webs of the brain, and the monstrous progeny of dreams, yet does it share with nature both those two grand tendencies; the one within the tranquil kingdom of custom and law, where, in a delightful repose and self-contemplation, it paints a series of quiet pictures: the other, in the violence of the whirlwind, the lightning, and the earthquake, by which the mother of all things quickly puts an end to those somewhile contradictions which are found in her works, in a manner which to us appears utterly lawless, though, in truth, conformably to her own immutable laws, by which she brings destruction out of life, and life out of destruction.

To demand of Goethe to give himself up exclusively to one of these tendencies, is at bottom nothing less than to require of him to cease to be Goethe ; which he could only accomplish by ceasing to acknowledge the laws of nature as the sole available rule for himself, and those like him. If then people have sometimes denied to this great and graceful genius a feeling for morality, it is because they have measured him by a standard which was inapplicable to him, and have not reflected that he could not love to make a sort of business of morality. In this, too, every thing not native and original, every thing merely learned by rote, was distasteful to him; as was all taught elevation of soul, all taught philosophy, all praying by rote, and so on. To such a degree was this the case, that he not unfrequently subjected himself to the greatest misinterpretation by expressing this aversion in the most undisguised manner, in the presence of men of flat and shallow minds. We shall see, however, hereafter, in the judgement he pronounced on Louis, King of Holland, and his brother, Napoleon, with what deep justice, truth, and gentleness, nay, reverence, he comprehended and regarded every tendency of a moral nature.

And if a rule of the English constitution, which declares that peers shall be tried by peers alone, may be applied to the moral world, such a recognition of the truly peculiar and noble on the part of so great a contemporary might shame and confound many a one-sided judgement, while it would substantiate what he says in "Tasso"—

> "——— wo du das Genie erblickst
> Erblickst du auch zugleich die Marterknone*."

* ——— Where thou beholdest genius
There thou beholdest too the martyr's crown.

CHAPTER III.

FAITHFULLY devoted to nature as Goethe was, he loved to speak of her works and ways with mysterious prefaces and intimations.

Thus he once led me to his cabinet of natural history and said, while he put into my hand a piece of granite which was remarkable for its unusual transitions, "There, take the old stone as a memorial of me. Whenever I find an older law in nature than that which manifests itself in this product, I will present you with a specimen of it, and take this back again. Up to the present time I have discovered none such ; and I doubt exceedingly whether any thing similar, not to say better, in this kind of phenomena, will ever come under my notice. Look attentively at these transitions : such is the universal tendency, the final result, of all in nature. Here, you see, is something which seeks another substance, forces its way to it, and, when united, gives birth to a third. Believe me, this is a fragment of the earliest history of the human species. The intermediate links you must find out for yourself. He who cannot discover them will not be the wiser though he were told them. Our scientific men* are rather too

* *Naturforscher*—investigators of nature.—*Transl.*

fond of details. They count out to us the whole consistency of the earth in separate lots, and are so happy as to have a different name for every lot. That is argil (*thonerde*); that is quartz (*kieselerde*) ; that is this, and that is that. But what am I the better if I am ever so perfect in all these names? When I hear them I always think of the lines in Faust—

'*Encheiresin naturæ* nenut's die Chemie
Bohrt sich selber Esel und weist nicht wie (9) !'

" What am I the better for these lots? what for their names? I want to know what it is that impels* every several portion of the universe to seek out some other portion, either to rule or to obey it, and qualifies some for the one part and some for the other, according to a law innate in

---

* See Goethe's conversation with me on occasion of Wieland's death, and especially what he so instructively discusses concerning Monads, or the ultimate simplest elements of all existences.

them all, and operating like a voluntary choice. But this is precisely the point upon which the most perfect and universal silence prevails."

" Every thing in science," said he at another time*, with the same turn of thought, " is become too much divided into compartments. In our professors' chairs the several provinces (*Fächer*) are violently and arbitrarily severed, and allotted out into half-yearly courses of lectures, according to fixed plans.

" The number of real discoveries is small, especially when one views them consecutively through a few centuries. Most of what these people are so busy about is mere repetition of what has been said by this or that celebrated predecessor. Such a thing as independant original knowledge is hardly thought of. Young men are driven in flocks into lecture-rooms, and are cram-

* February 9th, 1809.

med, for want of any real nutriment, with quotations and words. The insight, which is wanting to the teacher, the learner is to get for himself as he may. No great wisdom or acuteness is necessary to perceive that this is an entirely mistaken path.

"If the professor is master of a complete scientific apparatus, so far from mending the matter, it is all the worse. Then there is no end of the confusion and darkness. Every dyer at his copper, every apothecary at his retort, must come to school to him. The poor devils of practical operative men! I can't express how I pity them for falling into such hands! Once on a time there was a worthy old dyer in Heilbronn who was wiser than they all; but for that very reason they laughed him to scorn. What would I give that the old master were still in this world—the world which he knew, though it knew not him—and could see my Doctrine of Colours. That man's copper was his teacher ; he *knew* how things were brought to pass.

"If I were to write down the sum of all that is worth knowing in the various sciences with which I have employed myself throughout my life, the manuscript would be so small that you might carry it home in your pocket in the cover of a letter. We cultivate science, either as a means of gaining bread, or for the purpose of formally dissecting it in the lecture-room ; so that the only choice left to us poor Germans is between a shallow superficial 'popular philosophy,' or an unintelligible *galimathias* of transcendental phrases. The chapter of electricity is that which in modern times has, according to my judgement, been handled the best.

"Euclid's Elements still remain an unrivalled model of a course of scientific instruction. In their perfect simplicity, and in the necessary ascending gradation of the problems, they show us how all sciences should be entered upon and pursued.

"What enormous sums have been squandered by manufacturers in consequence of false notions of chemistry! Even the technical arts are very far from being as advanced as they ought to be. This book-and-closet knowledge; this wise-being, and wise-making, out of quires of stuff, copied from hand to hand, is the sole cause why the number of really useful discoveries is so small.

" If, on this very day, which we date the twenty-ninth of February, 1809, the venerable old English friar Bacon (who is by no means to be confounded with his namesake, Chancellor Verulam), after the lapse of so many centuries since his scientific labours, were to rise from the dead, walk into my study, and courteously ask me to make him acquainted with the discoveries which have been made in arts and sciences since his time, I should feel somewhat ashamed, and should not very well know what to answer the good old man. If it occurred to me to show him a solar microscope, he would instantly point to a passage in his works, in which he not only anticipated this invention, but paved the way to it by positive and practical suggestions. Should our conversation fall on the invention of watches, he would perhaps very composedly say, if I showed him mine, 'Aye, that's the thing; but it does not come upon me unexpectedly. In page 504 of my works you will find the practicability of such machines set forth; where I have likewise treated at length of the solar microscope and the camera obscura.'

"At last, after a complete review of modern inventions, I must perhaps expect that the deep-thinking friar would take leave of me in the following words:

" 'What you have effected in the course

of so many centuries is truly not so very considerable. Bestir yourselves better. I shall now lay me down to sleep again, and at the end of four hundred years more I will return and see whether you too are still asleep, or whether you have made greater progress in any branch of science !'

" With us Germans," continued Goethe, " all things go on very slowly. Twenty years ago, when I gave out the first idea of the Metamorphosis of Plants, in their criticisms on this work, people could find nothing to remark but the simple method of stating a scientific subject, which might perhaps serve as a very useful model to young people. Of the value of a fundamental law, from the developement of which (in case it were substantiated) every thing in the work followed, and which admitted of the widest and most manifold application to the works of nature, I never had the good fortune to hear a single word.

The reason is, that they can't find it in Linneus,—whom they transcribe and serve up again to their pupils.

" Every thing proves that men are made for Faith, and not for Sight. The time will come when they will believe in me, and quote me as authority for this and that. I had rather, however, they would assert their right, and open their *own* eyes, so that they might see what lies before them: as it is, they only mock at those who have better eyes than themselves, and are extremely offended if one accuses them of purblindness in their professorial views of things.

"The same remark is equally applicable to the Doctrine of Colours, which rests on one and the same principle as the Metamorphosis of Plants (10). They will however soon appropriate the results of these speculations. One must give them time,—and especially not take it ill when they pilfer what one does without acknowledging it (as has frequently happened to me in the Metamorphosis of Plants), and expose foreign wares as their own.

" As to Friar Bacon, extraordinary as was his appearance, it ought not to excite wonder in us. We know that rich germs of civilization showed themselves in England at a very early period. The conquest of that island by the Romans possibly laid the first foundation for its superiority. Such traces as they left are not so easily effaced as people think. At a later period Christianity made early and remarkable progress there. St. Boniface landed in Britain with a gospel in one hand, and a carpenter's rule in the other. He afterwards passed over to us in Thuringia, bringing in his train the arts of building. Bacon lived at a time at which the burgher class had already acquired important privileges by means of Magna Charta. The freedom of the seas, and of civil institutions, perfected what had been so happily begun. It was almost impossible that, under so many favourable circumstances, the sciences should remain in a backward state; that they should not also bound forward in the common race; which they truly did in the person of Bacon. This intelligent monk, as far removed from superstition as from unbelief, had a forecast of every thing, though he did not realise it. The whole magic of nature, in the noblest sense of the word, was opened to him. He saw all that was to come—that *must* come; the solar microscope, the clock, the camera obscura, the projection of shadows; in short, from the appearance of this one man might be inferred what mighty strides in the empire of invention, art, and science, the people to whom he belonged were destined to make.

" Press but ever onward," added Goethe with fervid animation, " youthful German people, and weary not in your progress on the way we have entered upon! Give yourselves up to no mannerism,—to no one-sidedness of any kind, under what name soever it finds its way among you. Know that whatever severs us from nature is false. The path of nature is that in which you must tread, if you would meet Bacon, Homer, and Shakespeare. On all sides there is much to do. See but with your own eyes, and hear with your own ears. Lastly, let not the hostility of men trouble you. We also have fared no better. In the centre of Thuringia, on the firm land, have we built our good ship; now are the floods come, and have borne it thence. Even now will many a one who knows the flat country wherein we moved, not believe that the floods have really risen to the tops of the mountains;—and yet of a truth are they there.

" Scorn not, in your efforts, to accept

the co-operation of like-minded friends; on the other hand, I exhort you (also after my own example) to lose no moment with men to whom ye belong not, and who belong not to you: for such can profit little, while in the course of our lives they may cause us many annoyances; and their intercourse is at best but vain and useless.

" In the first volume of Herder's ' Ideas towards a Philosophy of the History of Man' are many notions which belong to me, especially at the beginning. These subjects were at that time thoroughly discussed between us. What led to this was that I was always more disposed to an examination of nature through the senses, than Herder, who continually wanted to hasten to the result, and grasped at the idea while I had hardly got through the observation; but it was just this reciprocal stimulus that made us mutually profitable."

Another time—it was in the summer of 1809—one afternoon, I called on Goethe, and found him sitting in the garden enjoying the mild weather. Katz (10) the landscape painter, for whom he had a singular regard, was also there. Goethe set at a small garden table; before him stood a long-necked glass, in which a small live snake was moving about with great vivacity; he fed it with a quill, and made daily and minute observations upon it. He maintained that it knew him already, and raised its head to the edge of the glass, as soon as he came in sight.

" What splendid, intelligent eyes!" said he. " A great deal was half finished in this head, but the awkward writhing body would not allow much to come of it. Nature, too, has cheated this long, ensheathed organization of hands and feet; though this head and these eyes might well have deserved both. Indeed she frequently leaves such debts unpaid, at least for the moment, though sometimes she afterwards pays them under more favourable circumstances. The skeletons of many marine animals clearly show, that, when she made them, she was full of the thought of some higher race of land animals. Very often, working in an ungenial and intractable element, she was obliged to content herself with a fish's tail where she evidently would have liked to give a pair of hind feet into the bargain—nay, even where the rudiments of them are clearly to be discerned in the skeleton."

Near the glass which contained the snake, lay some chrysalids of caterpillars, whose forthcoming Goethe was expecting. They showed a remarkable mobility—sensible to the touch. Goethe took them off the table, watched them eagerly and attentively, and then said to his boy; " Carry them in doors; they will hardly come out today.

It is too late now." It was four in the afternoon.

At this moment Frau von Goethe came into the garden.

Goethe took the chrysalids out of the boy's hand and laid them again upon the table.

" How magnificent that fig-tree is, in leaf and blossom," exclaimed Frau von Goethe to us from a considerable distance, as she advanced towards us along the middle walk of the garden.

After greeting me and receiving my salutations in return, she immediately asked me, whether I had gone close to the fig-tree to admire it. " We will not forget," said she, at the same time addressing herself to Goethe, " to have it matted next winter."

Goethe smiled and said, " Let yourself be shown the fig-tree—and that directly,— or we shall have no peace this evening. And it really is worth seeing, and deserves to be handsomely dealt with and provided for."

" What is the name of this exotic plant," resumed Frau von Goethe, "which a man lately brought us from Jena?"

" Do you mean the great hellebore?"

" Yes, it thrives admirably."

" I am glad of it. We shall make a second Anticyra of this place, in time."

" There, I see, lie the chrysalids—have you seen nothing yet?"

" I laid them there for you. Do listen, I beg of you:" (taking them again in his hand and holding them to his ear) "how it knocks; how it jumps; and *will* burst forth into life. Wonderful would I fain call these transitions of nature, were not the wonderful in nature the most usual and ordinary. But we must not omit to let our friend here partake of this sight. Tomorrow, or the day after tomorrow, the butterfly will probably be here, and a prettier, more elegant thing you have seldom seen in your life. I know the caterpillar, and I summon you to attend tomorrow afternoon, at the same hour, in the garden, if you have a mind to see something more remarkable, than the most remarkable, of all the remarkable things, Kotzebue saw on his long journey to Tobolk, in the 'most remarkable years of his life*.' Meanwhile let us put the box in which our yet unknown, beautiful sylph lies enclosed, and decks herself in all her splendour for tomorrow, into a sunny window in the summer-house.

" So, there you stand, my nice, pretty child. Nobody will interrupt you in this corner, nor disturb you while you are completing your toilet."

" Well for my part," said Frau von Goethe, casting a side glance at the snake, " I could not endure such a nasty thing as

* " *Die merkwürdigsten Jahre meines Lebens.*" The title of Kotzebue's book.—*Transl.*

that near me, still less feed it with my own hands. It is such a disagreeable creature! It makes me shudder to look at it."

"Hold your tongue," replied Goethe, though tranquil as he was himself, he was generally not displeased at this vivacity of expression in those around him.

"Yes," added he, turning to me, "if the snake would but spin himself a house, and turn into a butterfly to oblige her, we should hear no more about "nasty things." But, dear child, we can't all be butterflies, nor fig-trees decked with flowers and fruit. Poor snake! they despise you! They should treat you better. How he looks at me! How he rears his head! Is it not as if he knew that I was taking his part? Poor thing! How he is pent up there, and cannot come forth, how fain soever he be! Doubly—I mean—first in the glass, and then in the scaly case in which nature has enclosed him."

As he said this, he began to lay aside his reed pencil and the drawing paper on which he had made some strokes towards a fantastic landscape, without seeming the least interrupted by the conversation.

The servant brought water, and while he was washing his hands, he said, " To return once more to Katz, the painter, whom you must have met as you came in ; the sight of him is most agreeable and refreshing to me.   He is exactly the same in every re-spect in Weimar as he was in the Villa Borghese.   Every time I see him, it is as if he brought a bit of the *dolce far niente* of the Roman atmosphere of art, into my presence.   As he is here, I will arrange a little scrap-book of my drawings.   We constantly talk a great deal too much. We ought to talk less and draw more.   I, for my part, should be glad to break my-self of talking altogether, and speak like creative nature, only in pictures.   That fig-tree, this little snake, the chrysalis that lies there on the window, quietly awaiting its new existence—all these are pregnant Signatures ; indeed he who could decipher them might well afford to dispense with the Written or the Spoken. The more I reflect upon it, the more it strikes me that there is something so useless, so idle, I could almost say so buffoonish in talk, that one is awe-stricken before the deep solemn repose and silence of nature, as soon as one stands withdrawn into oneself, and confronted with her, before some massive wall of rock, or in the solitude of some venerable mountain.

" I have brought together a number of varieties of plants and flowers," said he, pointing to the fantastic drawing before him, " strangely enough here, on this piece of paper. These spectres might be yet more wild and fantastic, and the question might still remain, whether the originals of them are not actually to be found in some part of the world or other.

" In design, the soul gives utterance to some portion of her inmost being; and the highest mysteries of creation are precisely those which, (as far as relates to their fundamental plan), rest entirely on design and modelling*; these are the language in which she reveals them.

"The combinations in this field are so infinite, that they afford a place even for the exercise of humour. I will take only the parasitical plants; how much of the fantastic, the burlesque, the bird-like, is contained in their fleeting characters! Their flying seeds perch like butterflies on some tree, and feed upon it till the plant is fullgrown. Thus, rooted in the very bark, we find the misseltoe, from which bird-lime is made, growing like a branch out of the

* *Zeichnung und Plastic.* It might be Englished, Outline and Form.—*Transl.*

pear-tree. Here, not content with fastening itself as a guest, it forces the pear-tree to supply its very wood out of its own substance.

" The moss on trees, which is also a parasite, belongs to the same class. I have some very fine preparations of this tribe of plants, which undertake nothing on their own account, but deposit themselves in all directions on something that comes ready to their hand. I will show you them at some favourable opportunity. Remind me of it. The peculiar construction of the rooty part of certain shrubs, which also belong to the parasitical class, is explained by the ascent of the sap, which is not drawn (according to the common course of nature) from a rude earthy matter, but from one already organized and fashioned.

" No apple grows from the middle of the trunk, where all is rough and woody. A long series of years, and the most careful training, are necessary to transform the apple-tree into a fruitful, succulent tree, sending forth blossom and then fruit. Every apple is a globular compact mass, and, as such, requires both a great concentration, and at the same time an uncommon refining and perfecting of the juices which flow into it from all sides.

" Figure to yourself Nature, how she sits, as it were at a card-table, incessantly calling ' *au double!* ' *i. e.* exulting in what she has already won, through every region of her operations ; and thus plays on into infinitude. Animal, vegetable, mineral, are continually set up anew after some such fortunate throws; and who knows, whether the whole race of man is any thing more than a throw for some higher stake."

During this agreeable conversation, evening had closed in ; and as it was grown too cool for the garden, we went up stairs into the sitting-room. Some time after, we were standing at the window. The sky was thick-sown with stars. The chords in Goethe's soul, which the open air of the garden and the works of nature had struck, still quivered, and during the whole evening their vibration was not stilled.

" All is so vast," said he to me, " that an end—a cessation of existence—is no-wise to be thought of. Or do you think it possible that the all-creating Sun may be entirely effete with the production of his own planetary system ; and that his earth-and-moon-creating power may be either entirely gone out of him, or lie utterly in-active and useless ? I can by no means be-lieve this. It appears to me extremely probable that, beyond Mercury, which is already small enough, a still smaller star will some time or other become visible. We see, it is true, from the position of the planets, that the projectile power of the Sun is notably decreased; since the greatest masses in the system are at the greatest distance from him. In this way, to pursue our inference, the time may come that the projectile force may be so exhausted, that the attempted projection of a planet may miss. If the Sun cannot sever and cast off the young planet to a proper distance, like its predecessors, he will, perhaps, have. a ring like Saturn's form itself around him, which being composed of earthy particles, would reduce us poor earth-inhabitants to a sad condition. And, indeed, the shadow of such a ring would produce a not very cheering effect upon all the other planets of our system. The genial influence of light and heat must naturally be greatly diminished by it, and all organizations whose development is their work, must in their several degrees be cramped and stunted by it.

" On this view of the subject, the spots in the Sun might certainly cause us some uneasiness for the future. Thus much is certain, that, at least, in all that we know of the past history and the laws of our own planet, there is nothing to prevent the formation of a solar ring, though, to be sure, it would be difficult to assign any time for such an event."

On calling on Goethe at three o'clock in the afternoon, I found him serious and thoughtful. He was busied in sorting a collection of coins.

To a true observer of nature like Goethe, it gave no little pleasure when he lighted upon a face among his coins, the features of which expressed the peculiar character or acts of the person, such as they are handed down to us by history.

With his collection of natural curiosities he went to work in the same manner. How to catch nature, so to speak, in the fact ;— this was the point to which all his observations, all his speculations, were directed.

The smallest object acquired importance and interest in his eyes, viewed from this side. Especially organic remains of a world which has partly perished.

Whoever wished to recommend himself to him for ever, needed only to bring him some such specimen from his travels. The paw of an arctic bear or of a beaver, the tooth of a lion, the strangely twisted horn of a chamois or a deer, or any other object differing in part or wholly from familiar forms and organizations, sufficed to delight him for days and weeks and to furnish him with matter for repeated observations.

When he obtained possession of such a treasure, it was as if he had received a letter from a friend in some far distant quarter of the globe; in the joy of his heart he immediately hastened in the most engaging manner to share with others its contents, which he had such singular felicity in decyphering.

He laid down the proposition, that Nature, accidentally, and as it were against her will, became the tell-tale of her own secrets. That every thing was told—at least once; only not in the time and place at which we looked for, or suspected it; we must collect it here and there, in all the nooks and corners in which she had let it drop. Hence the Mysterious, the Sybiline, the Incoherent, in our observations of nature. That she was a book of the vastest, strangest contents, from which, however, we might gather, that many of its leaves lay scattered around in Jupiter, Uranus, and other planets. To come at the whole, would be difficult, if not utterly impossible. On this difficulty, therefore, must all systems suffer shipwreck.

CHAPTER IV.

THIS same concatenation, which is only hidden from our short or purblind sight by its abundance and extent, and which Goethe traced in all the productions of nature with a loving and a divining eye, he also detected in the labyrinthine depths and forms of the spiritual world. As an illustration of his views, I make choice of two conversations with him; one on the immortality of the soul, and one on political institutions, as affording evidence how much the peculiar developement of his mind was in conformity with nature.

On the day of Wieland's funeral, of which I shall have occasion to speak more hereafter, I remarked such a solemn tone in Goethe's whole manner, as we were seldom accustomed to see in him. There was something so softened, I might almost say so melancholy, about him; his eyes frequently glistened; even his voice, his manner of speaking, were different from what was usual.

This might possibly be the cause that our conversation took a direction towards the super-sensual, for which Goethe commouly showed a repugnance, if not a contempt: completely on principle, as it appears to me; for it was more consonant with his natural disposition rather to confine himself to the Present, and to all agreeable and beautiful objects which nature and art offer to the eye and the observation, in paths accessible to us.

Our departed friend was naturally the principal subject of our conversation. Without deviating greatly from its current, I asked him on one occasion, when he spoke of the continuance of existence after death, as a thing of course, "And what do you think is at this moment the occupation of Wieland's soul?"

" Nothing petty, nothing unworthy, nothing out of keeping with that moral greatness which he all his life sustained," was the reply.

" But not to be misunderstood; as we have entered on this subject, I must go somewhat deeper into it.

" It is something to have passed a life of eighty years in unblemished dignity and honour; it is something to have attained to that pitch of refined wit, of tender, elegant thought, which predominated so delightfully in Wieland's soul ; it is something to have possessed that industry, that iron persistency and perseverance, in which he surpassed us all."

" Would not you willingly assign him a place near his Cicero, with whom he busied himself so cheerfully up to the time of his death ?"

" Don't interrupt me, when I am trying to give to the course of my ideas a perfect and calm developement. *The destruction of such high powers of soul is a thing that never, and under no circumstances, can even come into question*.* Nature is not such a prodigal spendthrift of her capital. Wieland's soul is one of Nature's treasures ; a perfect jewel. What adds to this is, that his long life had encreased, not diminish-

* These words are thus distinguished in the original. —*Transl.*

ed, these noble intellectual endowments. Again, I entreat you, think attentively on this circumstance. Raphael was scarcely thirty, Kepler scarcely forty, when they suddenly terminated their respective lives, while Wieland—"

" How," interrupted I with some surprise, " do you speak of dying as if it were a spontaneous act ?"

" That I often allow myself to do," replied he ; " and if you are pleased to consider it under a different aspect, I will (since at this moment I may be permitted to do so) tell you my thoughts upon the subject from the very bottom."

I begged him most earnestly not to withhold any of his opinions from me.

" You have long known," resumed he, " that ideas which are without a firm foundation in the sensible world, whatever be their value in other respects, bring with them no conviction to me ; for that, in what concerns the operations of nature, I want to *know*, not merely to conjecture or to believe. With regard to the individual existence of the soul after death, my course has been as follows :

" This hypothesis stands in no sort of contradiction with the observations of many years, which I have made on the constitution of our own species, and of all other existences ; on the contrary they furnish fresh evidence in its support.

" But how much, or how little, of this individual existence is worthy to endure is another question, and a point we must leave to the Deity. At present I will only make this preliminary remark. I assume various classes and orders of the primary elements of all existences, as the germs of all phenomena in nature ; these I would call souls, since from them proceeds the animation or vivification of the whole. Or rather *monades* :—Let us always stick to that Leibnitzian term ; a better can scarcely be found, to express the simplicity of the simplest existence. Now, as experience shows us, some of these monades or germs are so small, so insignificant, that they are, at the highest, adapted only to a subordinate use and being. Others, again, are strong and powerful. These latter, accordingly, draw into their sphere all that approaches them, and transmute it into something belonging to themselves ; *i. e.* into a human body, into a plant, an animal, or, to go higher still, into a star. This process they continue till the small or larger world, whose completion lies predestined in them, at length comes bodily into light. Such alone are, I think, properly to be called *souls*. Hence it follows, that there are monades of worlds, souls of worlds; as well as monades of ants and souls of ants ; and that both are, if not of identical, of cognate origin.

" Every sun, every planet, bears within itself the germ of a higher fulfilment, in virtue of which its developement is as regular, and must take place according to the same laws, as the developement of a rose-tree, by means of leaf, stalk, and flower. You may call the germ an idea*, or a monad, as you please; I have no objection. Enough that it is invisible, and antecedent to the visible external developement. We must not be misled by the *larvæ* or imperfect forms of the intermediate states which this idea or germ may assume in its transitions. One and the same metamorphosis, or capacity of transformation in nature, produces a rose out of a leaf, a caterpillar out of an egg, and again a butterfly out of the caterpillar.

" The inferior monades, too, belong to a superior because they must, not because it particularly conduces to their pleasure.

* Idea is here used in the Platonic sense.—*Transl.*

This takes place in general naturally enough. Let us observe this hand, for instance. It contains parts which are every moment at the service of that chief monas, which had the power, at their first rise into being, to attach them to itself. By means of them I can play this or that piece of music; I can make my fingers fly as I will over the keys of the piano-forte. They certainly thus procure me a delightful intellectual pleasure: but they are deaf; it is the chief monas alone that hears. I may therefore presume that my hand, or my fingers, are little, or not at all, interested in my playing. The exercise of monades, by means of which I procure for myself an enjoyment, is very little for the good of my subjects; unless, perhaps, that it tires them.

" How much better off they would be as to sensual enjoyment, could they, instead of idly roaming over the keys of my piano, fly about the meadows like busy bees, perch in a tree, or revel among its blossoms ; and doubtless the materials for all this exist in them. The moment of death, which is thence most appropriately called *dissolution*, is that in which ·the chief or ruling monas dismisses all those subordinate monades which have hitherto been faithful vassals in her service. I therefore regard the quitting life, as well as the rising into it, as a spontaneous act of this chief monas ; which, from its very constitution, is utterly unknown to us.

" All monades are by nature so indestructible that even in the moment of dissolution they do not abate or lose anything of their activity, but continue their progress uninterruptedly. They quit their old connections only to enter into new ones at the same instant. At the change, all depends upon the degree of strength of the germ of fulfilment contained in this or that mo-

nas. Whether the Monas be that of a
cultivated human soul, of a beaver, of
a bird, or of a fish, makes an immense
difference. And here, as soon as we desire
to explain to ourselves in any degree the
phenomena of nature, we come to the class
or order of the souls which we are compelled to assume. Swedenborg examined
into this in his peculiar manner, and em-
ploys an image for the illustration of his
thoughts, than which a more felicitous one
could not, perhaps, be found. He likens
the abode in which souls dwell to a space
divided into three main chambers, in the
centre of which is a large hall. We will
assume now, that out of these three chambers various sorts of creatures, as for instance, fishes, birds, dogs, cats, &c. repair
into the large hall ; certainly a very mixed
company ! What would be the immediate
consequence ? The pleasure of being together would soon be at an end. Sud-

den and violent friendships would give place to more violent quarrels; at length like would consort with like; fish with fish, bird with bird, dog with dog, and cat with cat; and each of these several kinds would endeavour, if possible, to get possession of a separate chamber. Here we have the full and true history of our monades, and of their departure from this earth. Each monas goes to the place whither it belongs; into the water, into the air, into the fire, into the stars; nay, the mysterious attraction which draws it thither, involves at the same time the secret of its future destination.

"Annihilation is utterly out of the question; but the possibility of being caught on the way by some more powerful, and yet baser monas, and subordinated to it,— this is unquestionably a very serious consideration; and I, for my part, have never been able entirely to divest myself of the fear of it, in the way of a mere observation of nature."

At this moment, a dog was heard repeatedly barking in the street. Goethe, who had a natural antipathy to dogs, sprang hastily to the window, and called out to it, "Take what form you will, vile larva, you shall not subjugate me!" A most strange and astounding address to any one unacquainted with the trains of Goethe's thoughts; but to those familiar with them, a burst of humour singularly well-timed and appropriate.

"This rabble of creation," resumed he, after a pause, and somewhat more calmly, "is extremely offensive. It is a perfect pack of monades with which we are thrown together in this planetary nook; their company will do us little honour with the inhabitants of other planets, if they happen to hear anything about them."

I asked him whether he believed that the

transition from their actual state and circumstances into others, were accompanied
with consciousness in the monades themselves.

To which Goethe replied; "That monades may be capable of a general historical
retrospect, I will not dispute, any more
than that there may be among them higher
natures than ourselves. The progress of
the monas of a world can and will elicit
many things out of the dark bosom of
its memory, which seem like divinations,
though they be at bottom only dim recollections of some foregone state; just as
human genius discovered the laws concerning the origin of the universe, not by dry
study but by a lightning flash of recollection glowing on the darkness; because
itself was a party to their composition.
It would be presumption to set bounds
to such flashes in the memory of spirits of
a higher order, or to attempt to determine

at what point this illumination must stop. Thus, universally and historically viewed, the permanent individual existence of the monas of a world appears to me by no means inconceivable.

" As to what more nearly concerns ourselves, it seems to me as if the former states or circumstances through which we and our planets have passed, were too insignificant and mean, for much of it to have been, in the eyes of Nature, worthy to be remembered again. Even the circumstances of our present condition would stand in need of great selection, and our chief monas will, at some future time, grasp the whole of it at once, and summarily; *i. e.* in one grand historic point."

This expression of Goethe's recalled to me something similar which Herder once said concerning the soul, when he was greatly out of humour and out of spirits with the world.

" We are now standing," said that immortal man, " face to face in the churchyard of St. Peter and St. Paul, and I hope we shall stand face to face in like manner in Uranus; but God forbid that I should carry with me the history of my sojourn here in these streets, lying on the Ilm, in all its minutest details! I, for my part, should regard such a gift as the greatest torment and punishment."

" If we give ourselves up to our conjectures,'" said Goethe, continuing his remarks, " I really do not see what should prevent the monas to which we are indebted for Wieland's appearance on our planet, from forming in its new state the highest combinations this universe can present. By its industry, by its zeal, by its high intellect, which enabled it to master so large a portion of the history of the world, it has a claim to every thing. I should be little surprised, inasmuch as I should find it entirely agreeable to my views of the subject, if thousands of years hence I were to meet this same Wieland as the monas of a world; as a star of the first magnitude; were to see him, and be witness how he quickened and cheered every thing that approached him by his beautiful light. To fashion the misty substance of some comet into light and clearness—that were truly a welcome, gladsome task for the monas of our Wieland; as indeed, speaking generally, if we suppose the eternity of the actual state of the world, we can admit no other destination for monades, than, as blessed co-operating Powers, to share eternally in the immortal joys of gods. The work of creation is intrusted to them. Called or uncalled, they flock together of themselves; on every way, from all mountains, out of all seas, from all stars;—who may stop them?—I am certain, as you here see me, that I have been there a thousand times already, and hope to return thither a thousand times again."

" Pardon me," interrupted I, " I know not whether I should call a return* without consciousness a return : for he only *comes* AGAIN who knows that he has been in the same place before. During your observations of nature, gleamy recollections, and points of light from another state of the world, at which your monas was perhaps itself a co-operating agent, may have burst upon you ; but all this rests only upon a *perhaps* ; I wish we were in a condition to attain to greater certainty on matters of such moment, than we can obtain for ourselves through dim divinations, and those flashes of genius which sometimes

---

* There is an awkwardness here from our half Latin word, for again- or back-coming. *Wiederkunft* is a compound of *again* and *coming*, and consequently in the next sentence may be severed for the purpose of analysis with perfect convenience. I am obliged to use two different words, which destroys the sentence.—*Transl.*

lighten the dark abyss of creation. If we can come no nearer to our object; were we only to figure to ourselves One Loving Chief Monas as the central point of creation, which ruled all subordinate monades of this universe, in the same manner as our soul rules the inferior monades subordinate to her?"

"Against this conception, considered as Faith, I have nothing to say," replied Goethe; "only I am accustomed to attach no extraordinary value to ideas which have no foundation in sensible perceptions. Aye, indeed, if we did but know the structure of our own brain; and its connection with Uranus; and the thousand-fold intersecting threads along which thought runs hither and thither. But then we should not be conscious of the flashes of thought till they struck. We know only ganglions, portions of the brain; of the nature of the brain itself we know as much as nothing. What then can we pretend to know of God? Diderot has been greatly censured for saying, If there *is* not a God, yet, perhaps, there will be one. According to my views of nature and her laws, however, one may very easily conceive of planets out of which the higher monades have already taken their departure, or in which they have not yet been called into activity. A constellation is required, such as is not to be had every day, to dissipate the waters and to dry up the land. As there are planets for man, there may just as well be planets for fishes or for birds.

" In one of our former conversations, I called man the first dialogue that nature held with God. I have not the least doubt that this dialogue may, in other planets, be kept up in a language far higher, deeper, and more significant. At present we are deficient in a thousand of the requisite kinds of knowledge. The very first that is wanting to us is self-knowledge; after this come all the others. Strictly considered, I *can* know nothing of God but what the very limited horizon of sensible perceptions on this planet affords ground for; and that, on all points, is little enough. Hereby, however, *it is by no means asserted, that, by this limitation of our observations on outward nature, limits are likewise set to our Faith. On the contrary, the case may easily be, that by the immediateness of divine feeling in us, Knowledge must necessarily appear as a patchwork; especially on a planet which, wrenched out of its connection with the Sun, leaves imperfect all observation, which therefore receives its full completion by Faith alone*.* I have already taken occasion to remark in the " *Farbenlehre*," that there are primary phenomena, which, in their god-like sim-plicity, we ought not to distrust and dispa-

* This passage is so marked in the original.—*Transl.*

rage by useless enquiries, but leave to Reason and to Faith. Let us endeavour to press forward courageously from both sides, only let us keep the boundaries which sever them rigidly distinct. Let us not attempt to demonstrate what cannot be demonstrated! Sooner or later, we shall otherwise make our miserable deficiencies more glaring to posterity by our so-called works of knowledge. Where Knowledge is full and satisfactory, indeed, we stand not in need of Faith; but where Knowledge falls short, or appears inadequate, we must not contest with Faith its rights, *As soon as we set out from the principle that Knowledge and Faith are not given to destroy each other, but to supply each other's deficiencies, we shall come near to an accurate estimate of the Right.*"

It was late today when I quitted Goethe. He kissed my forehead at parting, contrary to his custom. I was going down stairs in the dark, but he would not permit me, and held me fast by the arm, till he rang for some one to light me out. At the door he warned me again to take care of myself, and to be on my guard against the raw night air. Never, before nor after, did I see Goethe in a softer mood than at the time of Wieland's death.

His conversation of today contains the key to many of the most paradoxical, and at the same time most amiable parts of his so often misunderstood character.

The loss of Wieland rendered this last remaining friend dearer than ever to me. On my return home, I wrote down the foregoing conversation; and I worked it out into certain results which have remained not without the greatest influence on the course of my life, and which I will therefore annex as appendix to the dialogue I have here given.

It is then true, and even so extraordinary a genius as Goethe himself was constrained to make the humiliating admission, that all our knowledge on the planet we inhabit is mere botch-work ! All our sensible perceptions, in all the kingdoms of nature, though conducted with the profoundest acuteness and the utmost deliberation, can as little enable us to form a perfect idea of God and of the universe, as the fish in the abysses of the deep (even supposing him endowed with reason) could emancipate himself from the influence of his conceptions, formed in that region of fins and scales of which he is an inhabitant ; or, in his nether element, create to himself a complete and accurate picture of the human form.

The problem of life, if placed in Knowledge alone, must necessarily induce a sort of despairing Faust-like discontent. Restored to Faith, as to our proper element, to each, from the highest to the lowest, is allotted a circle of dignified activity, by means of which he becomes a free and co-operating portion of this magnificent whole. Nor does all that merits remembrance, in the future state of the soul, appear less worthy of notice in this view of the case. We thus soon arrive at this conclusion;—that the universal question is not only concerning a creation by art and science, but much rather concerning a creation by moral effects and actions, in strict conformity with that which the voice of heaven within us declares an indispensable duty.

To participate in the joys of creation, or in the plastic energy of nature, in the sense in which the aspiring and presumptuous Faust desired it, is not indeed granted to us here; this sphere is closed against us, and we have only to wait humbly: but another and a higher sphere of creation, in which we are ourselves both the material and the architect, is laid open to our illumined eyes;—the emancipation of the human race from a state of animal debasement

and confounding perplexity ;—the regene-
ration of those high and heavenly impulses
(restored by our own efforts to their true
origin) which, with mighty arms, raise us
to a heaven that seemed lost to us.

What a boundless field here opens itself! But also what a boundless struggle with antagonizing powers awaits us
in this career ! Even amid the hot press
of human passions, to receive the injunc-
tions of supernal love in a lowly heart and
a reverent ear ; to live and die to and for
our Faith ; and, when the deceitful world
totters beneath our feet, to hold fast on
heaven ; to be sure and steadfast in the way
pointed out to us by the compass within,
as the bird on his flight towards Memphis
or Cairo ; certain that, if there be anything
lofty, lovely, great, and of good report in
the world, on this way it must be wrestled
for, on this way it will be won.

The gentle humane temper—not the

Titan-like defiance—of Prometheus, is the right one.

> Ich dich ehren?
> Wofür?
> Hast du die Schmerzen gelindert
> Je des beladenen?
> Hast du die Thränen gestillt
> Je des geängsteten?
> Hat nicht mich zum Manne geschmiedet
> Die allmächtige Zeit.
> Und das ewige Schicksal—
> Meine Herrn und deine (11)?

In various ways has this passage been misunderstood. Unquestionably it is not to be denied, that the same flower which springs up full of loveliness and fragrance on the field of poetry, if injudiciously or perversely transplanted to another soil, becomes a noxious weed; especially where it takes root in a youthful mind, as a pervading principle in the field of practical endeavour.

An expression which a great poet may put into the mouth of a vicious, or passionately-excited character, is not to be regarded as truth. The predatory monades of the shark or the sword-fish, which, urged by a blind instinct, fall on one another in the depths of the sea, chase away each other's prey, and, accordingly as they are stronger or weaker, devour or are devoured, might, if they could attain to some insight into the practical part of their calling, be allowed to utter maxims like the following in full and perfect earnest:—

> " Denn Recht hat jeder eigene Charakter,
> Es giebt kein Unrecht als der Widerspruch*."

or,—

> " Und wenn es glückt so ist es auch veziehn,
> Denn jeder Ausgang ist ein Gottesurtheilt."

But man, to whom the higher laws and destinies of the world have been declared by immediate revelation, degrades himself to

---

* For every genuine character is right,
There is no wrong save inconsistency.

† And what succeeds is ever viewed with favour,
For prosp'rous issues are Heaven's own decisions.

a class far beneath him, when he adopts principles which the angel within him must repudiate.

If I would sum up all the admirable things Goethe said on this occasion concerning Knowledge and Faith, in the shortest possible space, I could find no better way of doing so than in his own profound and significant words :—

" Wer darf ihn nennen ?" &c. (12)

It is certainly not to be denied that Goethe's view of the history of the world strikes one as rather different from that usually taught in schools and compendiums. Thus, for instance, he regards the origin of states as something which, like every other product of nature, must unfold itself instinctively and without rule, out of some independently-existing germ ; to this indeed mountains, rivers, climate, and other circumstances, contribute their share. Political systems, he thought, availed as little as philosophical, whenever they were in opposition with nature.

A state can no more renounce its mountains and its rivers, than a man his character; or, in compliance with any abstract idea, prescribe to itself conditions destructive of its own being. Such perverse, absurd attempts are sure to bring their own punishment. It ought never to be forgotten that nature shows us, that it is not to the head alone, but to another part, held in less reverence by the public, that the regular hexagonal cells of the bee owe both substance and form.

The best capital cities are always those which have arisen piece by piece out of the necessity of the moment, or in the press of circumstances. Such a central point, in which the people of a tribe congregated around their king or queen, like bees around their monarch, is precisely the best; and this is most clearly proved by the experiment of capital cities which owe their origin, not to natural causes, or the inclination and convenience of the people, but are constructed after the plan of some ingenious architect. The former, notwithstanding their narrow streets and irregular architecture, have always something cheerful and attractive about them; while the others, in spite of all their regularity, after the first impression is worn off, never fail to leave a feeling of cold and repulsive monotony.

Goethe, as has been already remarked, loved nothing that was the fruit of mere study; nothing got by rote. He maintained that all systems of philosophy must form part of our affections and of our life*,

* *Alle* Philosophie *müsse geliebt und gelebt werden.* The paraphrase above is miserably diluted and feeble; the literal English is, " that all philosophies *must be loved and lived*;" the vigour and significancy of which I cannot preserve in any form of expression that would be usually acknowledged as English.—*Transl.*

if they are to acquire any sort of practical significancy. "But do people really *live* now-a-days?" added he. "The Stoic, the Platonic, the Epicurean, each must get through with the world after his own fashion; that is, indeed, the great problem of life, from which no one, be he of what school he may, is exempt. Philosophers can furnish us with nothing but outlines. How far these outlines suit us; whether we, according to our natural constitution and endowments, are capable of filling them up in the requisite manner, that is our affair. We must try ourselves, and most carefully examine all that we receive into our minds from without by way of nutriment; otherwise either we destroy our philosophy, or our philosophy us.

"Rigid temperance and moderation, such for instance as Kant's, demanded a philosophy suited to that his natural disposition. Read his life, and you will soon find, how nicely he contrived to take off the edge of his Stoicism, which would otherwise have stood in too sharp a contrast with our state of society ; how cleverly he accommodated it, and placed it in equilibrium with the world.

" Every individual has, in virtue of his natural tendencies, a right to principles which do not destroy his individuality. Here, or nowhere, is to be sought the origin of all philosophies. Zeno and the Stoics existed in Rome long before their writings were known there. That same stern character of the Romans, which fitted them to be heroes and warriors, and taught them to scorn every suffering, and to be capable of every sacrifice, necessarily secured a prompt and favourable hearing to principles which made similar demands on the nature of man. Every system, even Cynicism, may succeed in getting through with the world, as soon as the right hero

for the attempt does but present himself.
Only the Acquired and Artificial in man is
what is most apt to founder on contradictions; the Innate can always make its way
somehow or other, and frequently obtains
a complete and triumphant conquest over
all that is opposed to it.

" It is, therefore, no wonder that the refined, tender nature of Wieland inclined to
the Aristippic philosophy; while, on the
other hand, his decided aversion to Dio-
genes, and to all Cynicism, may be very
satisfactorily traced to the same cause. A
mind in which the sense of all grace of form
was instinctive, as in Wieland, cannot accommodate itself to a system which is a
continuous offence against that grace. We
must first be in unison with ourselves, before we are in a situation, if not wholly to
resolve, at least in some degree to soften,
the dissonances which press upon us from
without.

" I maintain that some are even born Eclectics in philosophy; and where Eclecticism proceeds from the inward nature of the man, that too is good, and I will never make it a reproach to him. How often do we find men who are from natural disposition half Stoics and half Epicureans! It would not astonish me at all if such men adopted the principles of both systems, and tried, as far as possible, to reconcile them.

" Very different is that vacuity of mind which, from want of all independent inward bent, like a magpie, carries to its own nest every thing that may chance to come in its way from any quarter, and thus places itself, like one essentially lifeless, out of all connection with the life-abounding Whole. All such philosophies are utterly dead and worthless; for as they proceed out of no results, so neither do they lead to any results.

" Of popular philosophy I am just as little an admirer. There are mysteries in philosophy, as well as in religion. The people ought to be spared all discussions on such points ; at least, they ought by no means to be forcibly dragged into them. Epicurus somewhere says, 'This is right, precisely because the people are displeased at it.' It is difficult to foresee the end of those unprofitable and unpleasing mental vagaries which have arisen among us since the Reformation ; from the time that the mysteries of religion were handed over to the people to be pulled about, and set up as a mark for the quibbling and cavilling of all sorts of one-sided judgements. The measure of the understandings of common men is really not so great, that one needs set them such gigantic problems to solve, or choose them as judges in the last resort of such questions. The mysteries, and more especially the dogmas, of the Christian religion, are allied to subjects of the deepest and most intricate philosophy; and it is only the positive dress with which it is invested that distinguishes the former from the latter. Thence it happens, that frequently enough, according to the position a man takes up, he either calls theology a confused metaphysic, or metaphysic a confused platonic theology. Both however stand on too elevated ground for human intellect, in her ordinary sphere, to presume to flatter herself that she can reach their sacred treasures. The interpretation of them to the vulgar cannot go beyond a very narrow practical circle of action.

" The multitude, however, are never so well satisfied as when they can repeat, in a still louder tone, the loud declamations of some few who give the cry. By this process the strangest scenes are produced, and there is no end to the exhibition of presumption and absurdity. A half-educated, '*enlightened*' man often, in his shallowness and ignorance, jests on a subject before which a Jacobi, a Kant, the admitted ornaments of our country, would bow in reverential awe.

" The *results* of philosophy, politics, and religion, ought certainly to be brought home to the people; but we ought not to attempt to exalt the mass into philosophers, priests, or politicians. It is of no avail! If Protestants sought to define more clearly what ought to be loved, done, and taught; if they imposed an inviolable, reverential silence on the mysteries of religion, without compelling any man to assent to dogmas tortured, with afflicting presumption, into a conformity to this or that rule; if they carefully refrained from degrading it in the eyes of the many by ill-timed ridicule, or from bringing it into danger by indiscreet denial, I should myself be the first to visit the church of my brethren in religion, with sincere heart, and to submit myself with willing edification to the general, practical confession of a faith which connected itself so immediately with action."

CHAPTER V.

THOUGH Goethe was habitually very cautious and temperate in the expression of his opinions in the presence of persons of uncongenial character and sentiments, it occasionally happened that, excited by some monstrous absurdity or other, he was carried away by that wild, passionate fancy which he pours forth in such rich profusion

in Werther, in the " Letters from Switzerland" (*Briefe aus der Schweiz*), and in the
" Fair at Plundersweilern" (*Jahrmarkt zu
Plundersweilern*).   He was then precisely
like the bear in Lili's pack :—

> " Kehr, ich mich um,
> Und brumm ————
> Und gehe wieder eine Strecke,
> Und kehr, dort endlich wieder um (13)."

Society, art, the court, poets, politics, reviews, philosophy, the universities, every
thing, in short, that was in any way connected with the inner and higher life (or at
least that could establish its claims to such
a connection by words and works), served
him as theme ; and he played upon them
from top to bottom of his whole gamut
of growls.

Nothing could be so delightful and amusing as to hear the all-sided man suddenly
become a thorough-going, one-sided partisan—an inveterate, narrow bigot.   In

these moods he seized the world by one corner, and shook and worried it in every direction; though usually he was so afraid of disturbing or ruffling any thing, that he took it up most delicately by all four corners.

At such moments, his boundless fantastic extravagance was most captivating; but there needed only the smallest fragment of prose—of which, alas, society affords but too luxuriant a crop—to check the course of this brilliant, dashing torrent.

I remember one occasion, when Wieland read us the Knights of Aristophanes, which he had translated for his Athenæum. We were assembled at the country house of the Dowager Duchess Amelia at Tiefurth (14). It was towards the end of autumn.

It happened that the reigning duke, who was returning from the chase, took his way through Tiefurth. He came in after the reading was begun. The evenings were chill, and there was a fire in the room. The duke, who came out of the fresh air, found it too hot and opened one of the windows. Some ladies, whose thinly covered shoulders were ill defended against the cold, sat close to the window. Goethe, observing that they suffered from the draft, instantly rose, approached the window with cautious tiptoe steps, that he might not disturb the reader, and softly shut it. The duke, meantime, had passed to the other side of the room, and his face was suddenly over-clouded when he turned round and saw how contumaciously his commands had been resisted.

"Who has shut the window that I opened?" said he to the servants of the house; not one of whom dared to cast so much as a glance at the culprit.

Goethe, however, with that arch, reverential gravity which is peculiar to him, and at the bottom of which often lies the most refined irony, stepped forward before his master and friend, and said, " Your Highness has the power of life and death over all your subjects. Upon me let judgment and sentence be pronounced." The duke laughed, and the window was opened no more.

––––––––

" There sits the monster in long sleeves, and laughs at me for being such a fool as to be out of humour with the world,—as if I did not know how things are ordered in it, and that every thing in it and upon it is covered with dirt."

With these words Goethe received me, as I walked into his garden one afternoon in August, and found him sitting in a white waistcoat, on a little grassplot, under the shade of some trees.

It was Friday; there was to be a performance at the theatre on the Saturday, and an actor who was to play had just sent in his resignation, which had thrown the whole piece into utter confusion. The lateness of the notice was the thing which especially annoyed Goethe, upon whose shoulders the actor had thrown the burden, as precipitately as he had gotten rid of it from his own. Every director of a theatre is bound, as is well known, to provide, first, that there is a regular performance, and, secondly, that the public are entertained with pieces of the highest merit.

" Such *avanies*," resumed Goethe, still somewhat angrily, (while he poured out a glass of red wine, and motioned me to sit by him on the bench,) " must I now endure with patience from people who, when they come into Weimar at one gate, are looking for another at which to quit it. For this, I have been for fifty years a favourite writer of that which you are pleased to call the German nation; for this, I have had seat and voice, for twenty or thirty years, in the privy council of Weimar—at last to be at the mercy of such fellows as these!

"The devil! That I, at my time of life, should suffer such a tragi-comedy to be played, and act the principal character in it myself, I never could have conceived nor dreamt! You will tell me, I know, that all theatrical affairs are, at bottom, nothing but dirt—for you have looked far enough behind the curtain—and that, therefore, I should do well to let the whole beggarly business go its own way as soon as possible: but I must tell you, in answer, that the intrenchment which a good general defends is also dirt; yet he must not turn his back on it, unless he would have his own honour trodden in the dirt. We are not, for that, to accuse him of any predilection for dirt; and so I hope you will acquit me of any such tastes, on the same grounds."

" Posterity, more just,"—I began ; but
Goethe, without waiting to hear what I was
going to say, interrupted me with unusual
rapidity and vehemence, " I will not hear
any thing of the matter ; neither of the
public, nor of posterity, nor of the justice,
as you call it, which it is hereafter to award
to my efforts. I hate my ' Tasso,' just because people say that it will " go down to
posterity ;" I hate ' Iphigenie ;' in a word,
I hate every thing of mine that pleases the
public. I know that it belongs to the day,
and the day to it ; but I tell you, once for
all, I will not live for the day. This is the
very reason why I will have nothing to do
with that Kotzebue, because I am fully determined never to waste an hour on any
man who I know does not belong to me and
I to him.

" Aye, indeed—if I could but manage to
write a work—but I am too old for that—
that would make the Germans hate and

revile me heartily for the next fifty or hundred years, and say nothing but evil of me
from one end of the country to the other,—
that would delight me inexpressibly! It
must be a glorious work that could produce
such an effect, on a public of so utterly
phlegmatic a temper as ours. There is
some character in hatred; and if we did but
make a beginning, and show some depth
and force of character, be it in what it would,
we should be half way towards becoming a
people. ' *They do not like me,*' (*Sie mögen
mich nicht*) the flat, lifeless, insipid word!
Neither do I ' *like*' them (*Ich mag sie auch
nicht*)*! I have never been able to content
them! If, indeed, my Walpurgis sack should
be opened after my death, and all the Sty-
gian tormenting spirits, till then impri-

---

* *Mögen* is the infinitive mood of the cognate of our
imperfect verb *may*. *Ich mag*, I may. The Germans
use it to express the least intense volition or inclination.
For instance, at table, Will you take fish? *Ich dank,
ich mag es nicht.*—*Transl.*

soned, be let loose to plague others as they have plagued me ;—or if people should chance to stumble on that passage in the continuation of Faust, in which the devil himself finds mercy and pardon with God; —that, I think, they would not forgive me in a hurry."

" For thirty years they have been sorely vexed and tormented in spirit by the broomstick on the Blocksberg, and the cat's dialogue in the witches' kitchen, which occurs in Faust, and all the interpreting and allegorizing of this dramatic-humouristic extravaganza have never thoroughly prospered. Really people should learn, while they are young, to make and to take a joke, and to throw away scraps as scraps.

" Yet even the clever Madame de Stael was greatly scandalized that I kept the devil in such a good humour, in the presence of God the Father. She insisted upon it that he ought to be more grim and spiteful. What will she say if she sees him promoted a step higher—nay, perhaps, meets him in heaven(15) ?"

" Pardon me," interrupted I, " you spoke just now of a Walpurgis sack. This is the first word I ever heard fall from your lips on the subject. May I know what that is ?"

"The Walpurgis sack," answered Goethe, assuming the stern solemnity of an infernal judge, " is a sort of infernal pocket, case, bag, or whatever you like to call it, originally destined for the reception of certain poems which had a near connection with the witch scenes in Faust, if not with Blocksberg itself. As often happens, its destination expanded itself; just as hell had at first but one apartment, but afterwards had limbo and purgatory added to it as wings. Every bit of paper that falls into my Walpurgis sack falls into hell; and out of hell, as you know, is no deliverance. Nay, if I were to take it into my head (and I am not ill inclined for it to-day) to seize myself by the forelock, and throw myself into the Walpurgis sack,—by my faith, what's in is in, and can never get out; even were it my own self. So rigorous, I would have you know, am I about my Walpurgis sack, and the infernal constitution I have granted to it. In it burns an unquenchable purifying fire, which, when it seizes its prey, spares neither friend nor foe. I, at least, would not advise any body to go very near it. I am afraid of it myself."

A specimen of the contents of this Walpurgis sack, and of Goethe's humour, may be seen in the following sketch of a scene which was suppressed in the printed copies of Faust.

As Faust is anxious to see and know the whole world, Mephistophiles proposes to him, among other things, that they should go and crave audience of the emperor. It is just the time of the coronation. Faust and Mephistophiles arrive safe and well at Frankfort. They are to be presented. Faust refuses to go, because he does not know what to say to the emperor, or how to entertain him. Mephistophiles, however, bids him be of good courage, promises to be at hand in time of need, to prompt him whenever the conversation halts, and, in case it is utterly at a stand, to take upon himself both his person and the conversation, so that the emperor can never know with whom he has, or has not, spoken.

Faust, after some hesitation, consents. They go together into the audience-chamber, and are actually presented. Faust, to prove himself worthy of this honour, calls forth all the talent and knowledge of which he is master, and discourses on the sublimest topics; but his fire warms himself alone—it leaves the emperor cold as ever. His majesty yawns repeatedly, and is just on the point of putting an end to the conversation. Mephistophiles perceives this at the exact moment, and comes to the aid of poor Faust, as he had promised. He instantly assumes his figure, and stands before the emperor, with mantle, and collar, and sword at his side, to all appearance Faust himself. He takes up the conversation exactly where Faust dropped it, only with very different, and far more brilliant success. He argues, dogmatizes, and twattles right and left, cross over and back again, into the world and out of the world, till the emperor is lost in astonishment, and assures the surrounding nobles of his court that this is a most profoundly learned man, and that he could listen to him for days and weeks without ever being tired. That at first, indeed, he did not display his talents, but, when he was once fully launched on the stream of conversation, nothing could be imagined finer than the manner in which he propounded every thing : so briefly, yet with such elegance and depth. He must acknowledge, as emperor, that he never found such a treasure of thought, knowledge of the world, and profound experience, united in one person,—not even in the wisest of his counsellors.

Whether his imperial majesty crowned this eulogy with the proposition that Faust-Mephistophiles should enter his service, or accept the post of prime minister, is unknown to me. Probably, however, Faust, for good reasons, declined the offer—if it was made.

———

On Easter Monday, 1808, I spent the evening with Goethe in a small select party. That is what he likes. On this occasion he put no restraint on his fancy, but gave it free course ; especially when we came to talk of the theatre and modern literature, which he compared with political events, and carried through his comparison with the most amusing and lively humour. " Piccolomini" had been acted on the Saturday ; on the following Thursday, after a long interval, " Wallenstein," was to follow.

" It is," said Goethe, " with these pieces as with the choicest wines ; the older they are, the higher does their flavour become. I make bold to call Schiller a poet, and a great one too,—though the latest rulers and dictators of our poetical world assure us he is none. Wieland, too, they say is nothing. The only question then is, who *is* anything ?

" A little while ago a literary journal in one of the two towns of Ingoldstadt or Landshut, I don't precisely know which, formally proclaimed Friedrich Schlegel (16) first German poet, and Imperator* in the republic of letters. God preserve his majesty on his new throne, and send him a long and happy reign! For all this, one would not answer for it that he has not some very rebellious subjects in his kingdom, of whom we have some" (casting a side glance at me) " even in our own immediate neighbourhood.

" The German republic of letters is however now as busy a scene as the Roman empire in its decline, when every body wanted to govern, and nobody knew at last who was really emperor. Almost all our great men live in exile; and every impudent suttler may become emperor when-

---

* I find myself constrained to use this word, as Goethe does, since there is no other that expresses his meaning. Emperor (*kaiser*) has acquired a totally different acceptation in modern Europe, and is inconsistent with our notions of a republic : General in Chief, or Commander, expresses but part of the functions of Imperator.—*Transl.*

ever he can gain the good will of the soldiery, or acquire any other sort of influence.

" A few emperors more or less is a matter not to be thought of in such times. There were once thirty emperors ruling together in the Roman empire. Why should we have fewer chiefs in our learned state? Wieland and Schiller are already formally dethroned. How long my old imperial mantle will continue to hang on my shoulders, it is not easy to predict; I do not know myself. I am determined, however, if it should come to that, to show the world that my heart is not set upon crown and sceptre, and that I can bear my dethronement with patience: for truly no man can escape his fate (17).

" But what were we talking of just now? Oh, of emperors! Good. Novalis (18), however, was none; though in time he might have become one, as well as other people. Pity that he died so young, and moreover that he conformed to the taste of his age, and turned Catholic. Already, as the newspapers assure us, young damsels and students make pilgrimage in troops to his grave, and strew flowers over it with lavish hands. That is what I call a promising beginning, and one which leaves good hope of future results.

" As I read but few newspapers, I always beg such of my friends as are at hand to give me notice whenever any important event of this kind—a canonization, or the like—takes place. I, for my part, am content that people should say all imaginable harm of me during my life-time; after my death, they will be the more likely to leave me in peace, as all the matter of defamation will have been exhausted before-hand, so that little or nothing will remain to be said.

" Tieck was emperor, too, for a time, but it did not last long; he was soon deposed.

They said there was something too Titus-like in his temper ; he was too mild and good-natured. In the present state of things, the empire requires a rigorous sway, and what may be called a sort of barbaric grandeur.

" Next came the reign of the Schlegels. Things now went on better. August Wilhelm Schlegel, the first, and Friedrich, the second, of the name, both ruled with becoming severity. Not a day passed in which some one was not sent into exile, or in which a few executions did not take place. Perfectly right ! Such rulers have from time immemorial been immense favourites with the people.

" A little while ago, a young beginner somewhere represented Friedrich Schlegel as a German Hercules, who went about with his club, and smote whatever stood in his way, to the death. For this meritorious deed, the aforesaid valorous emperor raised the young gentleman to the rank of a noble, and, without further preliminary, declared him one of the heroes of German literature. His diploma is made out; you may rest assured of it: I have seen it with my own eyes. Grants, domains, whole articles in reviews and magazines, written by intimate friends, are given without stint. Enemies are to be secretly kept out of the way; their writings are to be discreetly laid aside, and not produced at all.

" As we have a very patient public in Germany, a public that never ventures to read a book till it has been reviewed, this affair is not badly contrived.

" The best thing in the whole business is the uncertainty; *e. g.* a man goes to bed at night well and happy as emperor ;—in the morning he wakes, and finds, to his great astonishment, that the crown is gone from his head. I must confess this is a sad mischance. However, the head, in as

far as the emperor had any, sits still safely
in its place; and that I regard as so much
sheer gain. What an ugly thing it is, in
comparison, to read of the old emperors
who were throttled by dozens, and thrown
into the Tiber! For my own part, though
I may be dispossessed of throne and sceptre, I really look to die quietly in my bed,
here, on the shores of the Ilm.

" To return to the concerns of our empire, and especially of emperors. Another
young poet in Jena has died too soon (19).
Emperor, to be sure, he could not become;
but the post of prime minister, lord high
chamberlain, or something of the kind, he
might have attained to. If not, a place
always stood open to him as one of the
great heroes of the press. To institute
a chamber of peers, for which property
should be made a qualification, would certainly be no despicable plan in German
literature. If that young man had only

lived a few years longer in Jena, he might have become a peer of the realm before he knew where he was ; but, as it turned out, he died, as I said, too soon. That was certainly premature. One ought to take care (as the rapid march of our modern literature demands) to cover one's self as quickly as possible with fame, and as slowly as possible with earth. That is the fundamental rule to establish. The business is by no means accomplished by the publication of a few sonnets, and two or three almanacks. The literary friends of this young man, indeed, assured us, in the public prints, that his sonnets would long survive him ; I have not enquired into the matter since, and therefore cannot tell whether this predicdiction has been fulfilled, or how the whole affair stands.

" When I was young, I remember indeed to have heard sensible men say, that a single masterly poet or painter was often the growth of a century ; but those times are long past. Our young men know how to manage matters better ; and leap from one thing to another, according to the fashion of the time, so that it does one's heart good to see them.

"Their labour is not to be before their age, but to embody the whole age in themselves ; and when that does not succeed to their heart's content, they are immeasurably dissatisfied, and abuse the vulgarity of the public, which, in its sweet innocence, is delighted with everything.

"I had a visit lately from a young man who was just from Heidelberg ; I think he could not be much above nineteen. He assured me, in perfect earnest, that his opinions were all made up ; and that, as he knew what he was about, he was determined henceforward to read as little as possible, and to endeavour to develope his views of human life, unaided, by his own observations on society, without suffering himself to be diverted or hindered by the talk, the books, or the pamphlets of others. That's a glorious beginning! When a man starts from zero,. his progress must needs be striking!"

Thus playfully was Goethe wont to reprove the follies of the age. We shall hereafter see more of such humourous traits and pranks of his, but of a more practical kind.

CHAPTER VI.

*The Duke of Saxe Weimar.—Consequences of the battle
of Jena.—State of Weimar and of Germany.—Blü-
cher.—Napoleon's threats against the Duke of Wei-
mar.—Battle-scenes.—Pillage and conflagration of
Weimar.—Heroic conduct of the Grand Duchess
Louisa.—Espionage at the Grand Duke's table.—
Charges brought against him.—His leaning to Prus-
sian officers.—Herr von Ende.—Herr von Rühl.—
Herr von Muffling.—The Duke's visit to the Duke of
Brunswick.–Goethe's emotion on hearing these charges.*

THE noble Duke of Weimar had obeyed
the call of honour, and, on the 14th of October, 1806, had followed the banner of
Prussia. The battle of Jena, the loss of
which decided the fate of the whole of the
north of Germany, brought our little state
also into the greatest jeopardy. While the
result of this bloody tragedy slowly travelled across the mountains from Jena to
us, its last act was destined to be performed

on the evening of the same day, in the streets of Weimar itself. Tumult, conflagration, and a three days' pillage, soon appeared in the train of this fearful event. The French followed up their successes in the most brilliant manner. Magdeburg fell more rapidly than the emperor himself had anticipated. Blücher, indeed, fought with dauntless intrepidity in the marketplace, and the streets of Lübeck; but this prophetic foreshow of the heroic courage of the Prussians (which Napoleon, intoxicated with his success at Jena, either would not understand, or could not) had no power to produce any favourable change in the general aspect of affairs.

The Duke of Weimar, after his Residence* had already been invested by enemies, double in number his own troops, and his territory over-run on every side, set out

* The capital of the small states of Germany is called not *Hauptstadt* (capital), but *Residenz.*—*Transl.*

at the head of the royal* cavalry intrusted
to his command, which he led with equal
firmness and success across the Elbe. The
presence of so dauntless a chief saved this
corps amidst the universal confusion; for
despondency had now taken possession of
the bravest and the best; and the craven,
oft-repeated cry, that all was lost, drove
even the Prussians, spite of their tried valour and recollected triumphs, into flight,
even before the French appeared.

Let us not attempt to conceal this fact;
for our honour is now the greater, that it
was once so with us. If Blücher and the
Duke of Weimar were not blinded by this
mighty blaze of military triumphs; if they
did not, like the rest, instantly renounce all
attempts at further resistance, it was urged
against them, especially the latter (whose
state and subjects were placed under French
domination as soon as he was known to

* *i. e.* Prussian.—*Transl.*

have joined the enemy's ranks), as a rash and ill-timed defiance.

Even before the battle of Jena, the most violent threats against the duke were afloat. As soon as the French came to Weimar, it was said, they would not leave one stone upon another. The duke would lose his crown and sceptre as a punishment for having had the presumption to draw the sword against that mightiest of emperors, at whose feet destiny had laid a world.

Under these circumstances, it certainly seemed that we had little of a cheering nature to expect; and, indeed, all who could flee fled. Only the wife of the reigning Duke, Louisa, born Princess of Hessen-Darmstadt (20), stayed behind, alone in the palace. In the midst of her people, amid conflagration and pillage, this noble woman received the conqueror of the world with perfect calmness and self-possession; and the collected, serene majesty of a great and lofty female soul, which she opposed to him in this decisive moment, extorted, even from him, respect and deference.

Messengers from that fight, so big with consequences, came one after another into her presence, while it was yet undecided, and was contested with varying success on the high ground between Jena and Auerstädt, from morning till evening.

It was on the 14th of October of the year 1806, at half-past six in the morning, that the thunder of the artillery awakened the inhabitants of Weimar out of their sleep. The report came with the wind; all the windows in the houses clattered and shook, and universal consternation spread through the town. Young and old rushed into the streets, on the heights, up the towers, out at the gates; whenever the roll of the cannon, which grew nearer and nearer, permitted favourable conjectures to their hopes, or suggested unfavourable ones to their fears.

The face of events changed rapidly. Disordered troops of horse soon galloped through the town, and, in their hurried course, assured us the victory was ours. Then appeared a party of French prisoners, whom the people, and the soldiers left to guard the town, in their fancied triumph, would have maltreated, had they not been restrained by a provident law. But a noble Prussian officer would not suffer it. He took a *thaler* out of his pocket, and gave it to a wounded and bleeding French chasseur, saying " *Buvez à la santé de votre empéreur.*"

The French prisoners were followed but too soon by Prussian cavalry mortally wounded, hanging athwart their horses. The multitude were still occupied with this saddening spectacle, when several artillerymen, begrimed with the smoke of gunpowder, and stained with blood, with faces as if covered with black crape, rushed in a troop through the Kegelthor into the town, spreading alarm and horror wherever they went, by their terrific aspect: for the anxious expression visible on their marred and distorted features, as they looked around `from time to time, and the dreadful marks—gashes of the sabre, and stabs of the lance—which they brought with them from the field, told but too plainly that death was close at their heels. He was indeed at hand.

The Webicht, the avenues leading to it, as well as the high road from Jena to Weimar, was filled with a thousand-voiced war-cry, in which the rush and shock of steeds and horsemen, the roll of the drum, and the call of the trumpet, the tramp and the neighing of horses, were at times to be distinguished. The firing at length totally ceased: then came that fearful pause, in which cavalry, charging on the enemy's rear, breaks through his ranks and commences a noiseless carnage.

The French now planted a few guns on the heights above Weimar, from which they could fire into the town. It was a calm, bright October day. In the streets of Weimar every thing appeared dead. The inhabitants had retreated into their houses. Now and then was heard the boom of one of the guns posted at Ober Weimar. The balls hissed through the air, and not unfrequently struck the houses. In the intervals, the birds were heard singing sweetly on the esplanade, and the other public walks; and the deep repose of nature formed an awful and heart-appalling contrast with this scene of horror.

But I must break off, and resume the pencil for the completion of this gloomy picture, at another time and place.

The first who occupied the market-place

of Weimar were a party of French chasseurs; they were followed by a large body of infantry. Order and discipline were utterly out of the question. The work of plunder was systematically begun. The crash of doors burst in, the shrieks of the inhabitants, were heard on every side. I shall only add, here, that at seven o'clock in the evening, when the houses opposite to the palace were in flames, the light was so intense that people could see to read hand writing, both in the palace court and in the market-place. None could believe other, than that the French would execute their threats, and lay the whole town in ashes.

When, therefore, at this terrific crisis the report was suddenly spread, that the Grand Duchess Louisa was still in the palace, the effect which it produced on the hearts of the citizens was such, that, wherever a few met together, their despair and anguish were changed into rapturous joy.

How beneficently this noble picture of
princely and womanly courage and magna-
nimity wrought upon all hearts and minds,
from the highest to the lowest, at this junc-
ture ;—what it prevented, and what it held
together,—shall be dwelt upon in another
place ; for it is just, nay, (considering the
transitoriness of all human things) it is
most praiseworthy, to take care that She
who lighted us, as our beacon, in this fearful storm, should be held up as a model of
the lofty intrepidity and constancy of woman, and consecrated to the admiration of
the remotest posterity.

Meanwhile these circumstances produced a far different effect on the minds of
the French. The deeply-offended emperor
permitted, indeed, the duke's return to his
states, but not without the strongest marks
of suspicion and distrust ; so that the noble-minded, frank, sincere German was
from this moment surrounded with spies,

even at his very board. As my business often took me to Berlin and Erfurt, at this time, I had frequent opportunities of hearing remarks from those high in authority, which made me absolutely certain that they were laid before the emperor as the results of the register of the secret police kept there; and I consequently thought it my duty to make this known to the duke.

I put them into writing as I heard them, with the most literal exactness, and transmitted them through a high channel.

On this occasion, Goethe displayed so noble and beautiful a personal attachment to the Grand Duke, that I should have it on my conscience if I failed to give to the German public this leaf of the biography of its greatest poet.

It frequently happened, when I visited Goethe, that the eventful circumstances of the time (in which I was myself actively implicated; not, as I thank God, for the calamity, but in the cause of my country) were discussed by us on every side with circumspection, though without alarm. On the occasion I allude to, I was visiting Goethe in his garden, after my return from Erfurt, and the conversation fell on the burdens and oppressions of the French government. I read to him the facts I had learned at Erfurt, point by point, exactly in the same state as they were afterwards laid before the duke.

It was alleged, among other things, that the Duke of Weimar had lent four thousand thalers to General Blücher, whose hostility to the French was notorious, and who, after his defeat at Lübeck, had retired with his officers to Hamburg, where they were in the greatest difficulties. It was likewise universally known that a Prussian officer, Captain von Ende (now governor of Köln) had been raised to the post of Grand Marshal to the Grand Duchess. Now it was not to be denied, that the placing of so many Prussian officers, who were notoriously disaffected, in the civil as well as the military service, was very unsatisfactory to France. The emperor, it was said, would hardly acquiesce in, or endure, the formation of a tacit conspiracy against him in the very centre of the Rhenish confederation. Even for the post of tutor to his son Prince Bernhard, the duke had selected a ci-devant Prussian officer, Herr von Rühl (afterwards general in the Prussian service). Herr von Müffling, too, also an officer, and son of the Prussian general of the same name (now on the Prussian general staff) had been appointed president of one of the courts* of justice in Weimar, with a large salary. It was notorious that the duke was on terms of strict personal intimacy with him; such connections could, of course, answer no other end than to nourish that

* Laudes Collegium.

concealed rancour against France, which was inveterate enough without. It appeared that every means were industriously sought to irritate and call forth anew the anger of the emperor, who had already had enough to forget on the part of Weimar. The conduct of the duke was, at all events, imprudent in the highest degree, even supposing him to be guiltless of evil designs. As an instance of this, he, accompanied by Herr von Müffling, had visited the duke of Brunswick (21), the deadly foe of France, on his march to Brunswick, after the battle of Lübeck.

Goethe heard me, in silence, up to this point. His eyes now flashed with fire, and he exclaimed, " Enough ! What would they have, then, these Frenchmen ? Are they human ? Why do they exact the utterly inhuman ? What has the duke done, that is not worthy of all praise and honour ? Since when, is it a crime for a man to remain true to his old friends and comrades in misfortune? Is then the memory of a high-minded man so utterly nothing in their eyes? Why do they require from the duke to obliterate all the noblest recollections of his life—the seven years' war—the memory of Frederick the Great, his uncle—all that is great, and glorious, and venerable in the former condition of Germany, in which he took an active part, and for which he, at last, set crown and sceptre on the die? Do they expect that he is to wipe out all this, as with a wet sponge, from the tablets of his memory, like an ill-reckoned sum, because it pleases his new master?

" Does your empire of yesterday, then, already stand so immoveably stedfast that you are exempt from all, even the slightest, fear of participating in the changes of human things? Formed by Nature to be a calm and impartial spectator of events, even I am exasperated when I see men

H

required to perform the impossible. That the duke assists wounded Prussian officers robbed of their pay, that he lent the lion-hearted Blücher four thousand *thalers* after the battle of Lübeck,—that is what you call a conspiracy!—that seems to you a fit subject for reproach and accusation!

"Let us suppose the case, that today or tomorrow misfortune befell your grand army;—what would a general or field-marshal be worth in the emperor's eyes, who would act precisely as our duke has acted under these circumstances? I tell you the duke *shall* act as he acts! He *must* act so! He would do great injustice if ever he acted otherwise! Yes,—and even were he thus to lose country and subjects, crown and sceptre, like his ancestor the unfortunate John, yet must he not deviate one hand's breadth from this noble manner of thinking, and from that which the duty of a man and a prince prescribes in such an emergency.

"Misfortune! what is misfortune? This is a misfortune;—that a prince should be compelled to endure such things from foreigners. And if it came to the same pass with him as formerly with his ancestor Duke John; if his ruin were certain and irretrievable, let not that dismay us: we will take our staff in our hands and accompany our master in his adversity, as old Lucas Kranach did(22); we will never forsake him. The women and children, when they meet us in the villages, will cast down their eyes, and weep, and say one to another, ' That is old Goethe and the former duke of Weimar, whom the French emperor drove from his throne because he was so true to his friends in misfortune; because he visited his uncle, the duke of Brunswick, on his death-bed; because he would not let his old comrades and brothers-in-arms starve!'"

At this, the tears rolled in streams down

H 2

his cheeks. After a pause, having recovered himself a little, he continued, " I will sing for bread! I will turn strolling ballad-singer* and put our misfortunes into verse! I will wander into every village, and into every school, wherever the name of Goethe is known; I will sing† the dishonour of Germany, and the children shall learn the song of our shame till they are men; and thus shall they sing my master upon his throne again and your's off his!

" Yes, mock at all laws—through them

---

* " *Bünkel Sänger*,"—*i. e.* a man who sings on benches at the doors of alehouses—the meanest and humblest of itinerant musicians.—*Transl.*

† I am much tempted to use here the true and perfectly English translation of the original *besingen*; since the difference between I will *sing* (it may be only once) and I will *besing*, is important. It is extremely to be regretted that we have let foolish and tyrannous custom confine this useful mode of forming a frequentative verb, or of modifying its sense in other ways not to be analysed here, to some three or four words, instead of applying it systematically and analogically to all, as the Germans do.—*Transl.*

at last shall you be brought to shame!
Come on, Frenchman! Here, or nowhere,
is the place to grapple with you! If you
seek to root out this feeling from German
hearts, or to tread it under foot, (which
comes to the same thing) *you* will soon be
under the feet of this very people.

" You see, I tremble hand and foot! It
is long since I was so moved.

" Give me this report! But no, take it
yourself! Throw it in the fire! Burn it;
and when you have burnt it, gather up the
ashes and throw them into the water! Let
them seethe, and stew, and boil. I will bring
wood myself for the fire, till it is utterly
stewed away;—till the smallest letter—
every comma and every point,—goes off in
smoke and steam, so that there remains
not an atom of it upon German ground.
And thus must we do with these insolent,
over-bearing strangers, if ever things should
go better with Germany."

I need not add a word to this truly manly burst of feeling, which did equal honour to Goethe and to the duke.

As I embraced Goethe, at taking leave, my eyes, too, were filled with tears.

NOTES.

NOTE 1.

THE Life of Curran, by his son, contains the following passage :

" His mother, whose maiden name was Philpot, belonged to a family well known and respected, and of which the descendants continue in the class of gentry. She was a woman of a strong original understanding, and of admitted superiority in the circles where she moved. In her latter years, the celebrity of her son rendered her an object of additional attention and scrutiny; and the favourers of the opinion that talent is hereditary thought they could discover, in the bursts of irregular eloquence that escaped her, the first visible gushings of the stream which, expanding as it descended, at length attained a force and grandeur that incited the admirer to explore its source. This persuasion Mr. Curran himself always fondly che-

rished :—'The only inheritance' (he used to say)
'that I could boast of from my poor father, was
the very scanty one of an unattractive face and
person, like his own; and if the world has ever
attributed to me something more valuable than
face or person, or than earthly wealth, it was that
another and a dearer parent gave her child a portion from the treasure of her mind.' He attributed much of his subsequent fortune to the early
influence of such a mother, and to his latest hour
would dwell with grateful recollection upon the
wise counsel, upon the lessons of honourable ambition, and of sober masculine piety, which she
enforced upon the minds of her children. She was
not without her reward. She lived to see the
dearest of them surpassing every presage, and ac-
cumulating public honours upon a name which she
in her station had adorned by her virtues."—*Life
of Curran, by his Son,* p. 4.

The mother of the Schlegels is said to have
been a remarkable woman, and to have contributed
greatly to form the character of her accomplished
sons.

In our own country examples enough in support of this theory might be found. Canning and
Brougham are the most recent I remember.

NOTE 2.

Georg Melchior Krause was born in 1733, at Frankfort on the Main, and was a pupil of the celebrated Tischbein. He studied for five years in Paris. In 1775 he was appointed Director of the free School of Design at Weimar, a post which he retained up to the time of his death, November, 1806. He died in consequence of the brutal treatment he received from some French soldiers, who burst into his house after the battle of Jena. He accompanied Gore the English traveller, who resided at Weimar, on a tour through Tyrol and the north of Italy. Gore and Krause were also with Goethe at the siege of Mainz, in 1793, and there is in existence a coloured engraving of the siege by Krause. Goethe says in the *Campagne in Frankreich*, 1793, " The siege of Mainz, as an extraordinary event *in which calamity itself promised to be picturesque*, enticed my two friends thither," *&c.* Gore, who seems to have been a great favourite with Goethe, was the original of his exquisitely finished portrait of the travelled Englishman, in the *Wahlverwandschaften*.

Krause used to work up for Goethe his pictorial fancies, some of which were extremely curious and wild. Some notice of them may be found among other interesting matter in the series of papers on Goethe's works which have lately appeared in the Monthly Repository.

I have found no other mention of Krause in Goethe's works than the following, in the *Zweyter Aufenthalt in Rom,* February, 1788. Just after the celebrated description of the carnival, he says that, as a memorial of the scene, he had employed his countryman Georg Schütz to draw and colour all the masks he could obtain. "These drawings," he adds, " were afterwards engraved and coloured after the originals, by Melchior Krause, of Frankfurt on the Main, Director of the free Academy of Design at Weimar."

NOTE 3.

In Goethe's *Tag-und-Jahres Hefte* (a sort of literary journal), A. D. 1802, I find the following notice of the death of this charming woman and actress :—" But while art flourished on our stage in all the freshness and activity of youth, a death occurred among us which I think it a duty to record.

" Corona Schroeder* died, and as I did not feel in a state of mind to consecrate to her memory a tribute worthy of her merits, I thought with great satisfaction, and a sort of wonder, that so many years ago I had erected a monument to her, than which I could not now even design anything more characteristic. It was on occasion of another death, that of Mieding, the stage decorator ; and was written in a tone of serious cheerfulness, if I may so speak, for my beautiful friend. Well do I remember this monody, neatly written out on black-edged paper for the Tieffurt Journal. It was, however, of no ill omen to Corona ; her lovely person, her gay joyous spirit, remained unbroken for many years. She should have staid longer to adorn and delight a world from which she retired too soon."

The following is the passage from the poem called *Miedings Tod*, in which Goethe has so beautifully, and as he says " characteristically," enshrined her memory.

I have hesitated long whether, as I cannot write verse, I should subjoin any translation of this and other poems. I am advised to risk the pub-

* So spelt in the original.—*Transl.*

lication of such as I can give, for the convenience of those who do not read German. It would give me extreme pain that they should be regarded as intended in any degree to represent Goethe's poems. They are intended merely to illustrate the text by showing what is the *matter* of those poems. It is so obvious that they pretend to nothing but fidelity—I might say literalness—that any apology for them would seem to me like soliciting criticism, of which they are not deserving. I have followed the verse, as nearly as possible, line for line; but to remove any appearance of pretension to a rhythmical form I have not put capitals at the beginning of the lines. This extract, the original of which is in heroic measure, is, I think, by far the worst specimen. In some unrimed metres it will perhaps be found that the English takes the form and colour of the German more easily.

Extract from " *Miedings Tod.*"

Ihr Freunde, Platz! Weicht einen kleinen Schritt!
Seht, wer da kommt und festlich näher tritt?
Sie ist es selbst, die Gute fehlt uns nie,
Wir sind erhört, die Musen senden sie.
Ihr kennt sie wohl: sie ist's, die stets gefällt;
Als eine Blume zeigt sie sich der Welt:

Zum Muster wuchs das schöne Bild empor,
Vollendet nun, sie ist's und stellt es vor.
Es gönnten ihr die Musen jede Gunst,
Und die Natur erschuf in ihr die Kunst,
So häuft sie willig jeden Reiz auf sich,
Und selbst dein Name ziert, CORONA, dich.
   Sie tritt herbei.   Seht sie gefällig stehn!
Nur absichtslos, doch wie mit Absicht schön.
Und hoch erstaunt, seht ihr in ihr vereint
Ein Ideal, das Künstlern nur erscheint.
   Anständig führt die leis' erhobne Hand
Den schönsten Kranz, umknüpft von Trauerband.
Der Rose frohes, volles Angesicht,
Das treue Veilchen, der Narcisse Licht,
Vielfält'ger Nelken, eitler Tulpen Pracht,
Von Mädchenhand geschickt hervorgebracht,
Durchschlungen von der Myrte santer Zier,
Vereint die Kunst zum Trauerschmucke hier:
Und durch den schwarzen, leichtgeknüpften Flor
Sticht eine Lorbeerspitze still hervor.
   Es schweigt das Volk.   Mit Augen voller Glanz
Wirft sie ins Grab den wohlverdienten Kranz.
Sie öffnet ihren Mund, und lieblich fliesst,
Der weiche Ton der sich ums Herz ergiesst.
Sie spricht: den Dank für das, was du gethan,
Geduldet, nimm, du Abgeschiedner, an!
Der Gute, wie der Böse, müht sich viel,
Und beide bleiben weit von ihrem Ziel.
Dir gab ein Gott in holder, steter Kraft
Zu deiner Kunst die ew'ge Leidenschaft.

Sie war's, die dich zur bösen Zeit erhielt,
Mit der du Krank, als wie ein Kind, gespielt,
Die auf den blassen Mund ein Lächeln rief,
In deren Arm dein müdes Haupt entschlief!
Ein jeder, dem Natur ein gleiches gab,
Besuche pilgernd dein bescheiden Grab!
Fest steh dein Sarg in wohlgegönnter Ruh',
Mit lockrer Erde deckt ihn leise zu;
Und sanfter, als des Lebens, liege dann
Auf dir des Grabes Bürde, guter Mann!

TRANSLATION.

Room, friends;—give way a little space.
See who comes, approaching with solemn step.
'Tis she herself!   The sweet one fails us never;
our prayers are heard; the Muses send her.
You know her well—know her unvarying charm;
like a bright flower she blossoms to the world!
The exquisite form grew up as a model;
consummate now, she presents herself as one before us.
On her the Muses lavished all their gifts,
and Art, in her, is Nature's own work.
Thus easily does she appropriate every charm;
and e'en thy name, CORONA, adorns thee.
    She steps forward.   See her attractive grace!
Without design—yet, as if with design, beautiful;

and, wondering, you see in her combined
an Ideal such as appears only to the artist's fancy.
   Gracefully does the softly-raised hand present
the fairest wreath, entwined with mourning bands;
the glad, full countenance of the rose,
the faithful violet, the bright narcissus,
the dappled pink, the splendour of the vain tulip,
skilfully grouped by maiden hands,
and blended with the softer grace of the myrtle,
Art here entwines as a funereal ornament;
and through the black, transparent crape
the laurel silently peeps forth.
   The people are silent! With bright, beaming eyes
she throws into the grave the well-earned wreath.
She opens her lips, and sweetly gushes forth
that liquid tone which pours itself around the heart.
She speaks! The thanks for that which thou hast
      done
or suffered, accept, Oh thou departed!
The good man, like the bad, toils wearily,
and both remain far from the wished-for goal.
Some God gave thee, in kindly, constant force,
the imperishable passion for thine art.
This was it that sustained thee in evil times;
this was it that thou play'dst with like a child;
which called a smile up on thy pallid lips;
in whose arms thy weary head reposed.
Let every one to whom Nature has given the like
visit thy modest grave in pilgrimage.

Untroubled be thy bier in well-earned peace.
With light earth cover it gently ;
and, softer than that of life, lie on thee
the burden of the grave, thou worthy man !

Goethe received the intelligence of Corona
Schroeter's death in Switzerland. His tender
regrets for his lovely, intelligent, and affectionate
pupil are exquisitely expressed in his *Euphrosyne.*
I must resist the temptation of inserting the whole
poem. The following lines are a specimen of it :

Sieh, die Scheidende zieht durch Wald und grauses
   Gebirge,
Sucht den wandernden Mann, ach! in der Ferne noch auf ;
Sucht den Lehrer, den Freund, den Vater ; blicket noch
   einmal
Nach dem leichten Gerüst irdischer Freuder zurück.
Lass mich der Tage gedenken, da mich, das Kind, du
   dem Spiele
Jener täuschenden Kunst reizender Musen geweiht.
Lass mich den Stunde gedenken, und jedes kleineren
   Umstands.
Ach, wer ruft nicht so gern unwiederbringliches an !
Jenes süsse Gedränge der leichtesten irdischen Tage,
Ach wer schätzt ihn genug, diesen vereilenden Werth !
Klein erscheinet es nun, doch ach ! nicht kleinlich dem
   Herzen ;
Macht die Liebe, die Kunst, jegliches Kleine doch gross.

TRANSLATION.

See the departing one comes, through forests, and over frightful mountains ; seeks out the wanderer, alas ! at a distance ; seeks her teacher, her friend, her father : once more turns her eyes back to the light fabric of earthly joys. " Let me think on the days when thou devotedst me, a child, to the exercise of that illusive art of the enchanting Muse. Let me think on the hour, and on every smallest circumstance—Ah ! who loves not thus to recall the irrevocable ? That sweet throng of the lightsomest earthly days—who prizes it enough— that swift-fleeting value ? Little seems it now—but oh not trifling to the heart ! Love, Art, makes each smallest thing great.

Note 4.

Goethe says, in his *Tag-und-Jahres Hefte*, A. D. 1790, " I found some compensation for the want of objects of art, in the observation of nature, and the study of a wide field of science. The *Metamorphose der Pflanzen* (Metamorphosis of Plants) was written to lighten my heart. I hoped, by publishing it, to afford to scientific men a *specimen pro loco*. A botanic garden was planned.

" Picturesque colouring was, at the same time, one of my objects of study, and, on recurring to the first physical elements of this branch of science, I discovered, to my great astonishment, that *the Newtonian hypothesis was false, and would not hold*. More accurate investigation only confirmed me in my persuasion, and thus I was inoculated with a fever for discovery, which had the greatest influence on my future life and pursuits."

In 1793, he says (after mentioning the first conception of his inimitable version of *Reinecke Fuchs*), " The *Farbenlehre* (Theory of Colours), too, accompanied me to the Rhine, and in the open air, under a bright sky, I continually gained fresh views concerning the various conditions under which colour appears.

" This variety, compared with my limited capacity of observation, comprehension, arrangement, and combination, suggested to me the necessity of a society. I thought out such an one in all its details ; marked out the objects to be pursued, and finally showed in what manner we might soonest co-operate to the attainment of our end. This project I laid before my brother-in-law, Schlosser, whom I met in Heidelberg, following the victorious army after the surrender of Mainz. I was most unpleasantly surprised when this veteran man of practice burst into a hearty laugh at me, and declared that, in the world generally, and in our dear German fatherland particularly, a common, disinterested co-operation in an object of pure science was not to be thought of. I, on the other hand, though no longer young, maintained my ground like a true believer; whereupon he told me many particulars which I then rejected, but of which I have since had experience more than enough. And so I, for my own part, held fast to these studies, as to a plank in a shipwreck; for I had now, for two years, personally and directly experienced the most dreadful disruption of all ties. One day in head-quarters at home, and one day in conquered Mainz, were symbols of the actual history of the world*."

In 1797, after mentioning the publication of *Hermann und Dorothea*, he adds, " I wrote the new *Pausanias* and the *Metamorphose der Pflanzen* in elegiac form." This beautiful poem I subjoin, with a literal translation.

* See another account of this same interview in the *Campagne in Frankreich.*

Die Metamorphose der Pflanzen.

Dich verwirret, Geliebte, die tausendfältige Mischung
  Dieses Blumengewühls über dem Garten umher;
Viele Namen hörest du an, und immer verdränget
  Mit barbarischem Klang einer den andern im Ohr.
Alle Gestalten sind ähnlich, und keine gleichet der
    andern;
  Und so deutet das Chor auf ein geheimes Gesetz,
Auf ein heiliges Räthsel.   O, könnt 'ich dir, liebliche
    Freundin,
  Ueberliefern sogleich glücklich das lösende Wort!—
Werdend betrachte sie nun, wie nach und nach sich die
    Pflanze
  Stufenweise geführt, bildet zu Blüthen und Frucht.
Aus dem Samen entwickelt sie sich, sobald ihn der Erde
  Stille befruchtender Schoos hold in das Leben entlässt,
Und dem Reize des Lichts, des heiligen, ewig bewegten,
  Gleich den zärtesten Bau keimender Blätter empfiehlt.
Einfach schlief in dem Samen die Kraft; ein begin-
    neudes Vorbild
  Lag, verschlossen in sich, unten die Hülle gebeugt,
Blatt und Wurzel und Keim, nur halb geformet und
    farblos;
  Trocken erhält so der Kern ruhiges Leben bewahrt;
Quillet strebend empor, sich milder Feuchte vertrauend,
  Und erhebt sich vogleich aus der umgebenden Nacht.
Aber einfach bleibt die Gestalt der ersten Erscheinung;

Und so bezeichnet sich auch unter den Pflanzen das
Kind.
Gleich darauf ein folgender Trieb, sich erhebend, erneuet,
Knoten auf Knoten gethürmt, immer das erste Gebild.
Zwar nicht immer das gleiche; denn mannigfaltig
erzeugt sich,
Ausgebildet, du siehst's, immer das folgende Blatt,
Ausgedehnter, gekerbter, getrennter in Spitzen und
Theile,
Die verwachsen vorher ruhten im untern Organ.
Und so erreicht es zuerst die höchst bestimmte Vollen-
dung,
Die bei manchem Geschlecht dich zum Erstaunen
bewegt.
Viel gerippt und gezackt, auf mastig strotzender Fläche,
Scheinet die Fülle des Triebs frei und unendlich zu
seyn.
Doch hier hält die Natur, mit mächtigen Händen, die
Bildung
An, und lenket sie sanft in das Vollkommnere hin.
Mässiger leitet sie nun den Saft, verengt die Gefässe,
Und gleich zeigt die Gestalt zärtere Wirkungen an.
Stille zieht sich der Trieb der strebenden Ränder
zurücke,
Und die Rippe des Stiels bildet sich völliger aus.
Blattlos aber und schnell erhebt sich der zärtere Stengel,
Und ein Wundergebild zieht den Betrachtenden an.
Rings im Kreise stellet sich nun, gezählet und ohne
Zahl, das kleinere Blatt neben dem ähnlichen hin.

Um die Achse gedrängt, entscheidet der bergende Kelch
    sich
  Der zur höchsten Gestalt farbige Kronen entlässt.
Also prangt die Natur in hoher, voller Erscheinung,
  Und sie zeiget, gereiht, Glieder an Glieder gestuft.
Immer erstaunst du auf's neue, so bald sich am Stengel
    die Blume
  Ueber dem schlanken Gerüst wechselnder Blätter
    bewegt.
Aber die Herrlichkeit wird des neuen Schaffens Ver-
    kündung.
  Ja, das farbige Blatt fühlet die göttliche Hand,
Und zusammen zieht es sich schnell; die zärtesten
    Formen,
  Zwiefach streben sie vor, sich zu vereinen bestimmt.
Traulich stehen sie nun, die holden Paare, beisamen,
  Zahlreich ordnen sie sich um den geweihten Altar.
Hymen schwebet herbei, und herrliche Düfte, gewaltig,
  Strömen süssen Geruch, alles belebend, umher.
Nun vereinzelt schwellen sogleich unzählige Keime,
  Hold in den Mutterschoos schwellender Früchte ge-
    hüllt.
Und hier schliesst die Natur den Ring der ewigen Kräfte;
  Doch ein neuer sogleich fasset den vorigen an,
Dass die Kette sich fort durch alle Zeiten verlänge,
  Und das Ganze belebt, so wie das Einzelne sey.
Wende nun, o Geliebte, den Blick zum bunten Gewim-
    mel,
  Das verwirrend nicht mehr sich vor dem Geiste bewegt.

Jede Pflanze verkündet dir nun die ew'gen Gesetze,
  Jede Blume, sie spricht lauter und lauter mit dir.
Aber entzifferst du hier der Göttin heilige Lettern,
  Ueberall siehst du sie dann, auch in verändertem Zug.
Kriechend zaudre der Raupe, der Schmetterling eile
  geschäftig,   [stalt.
  Bildsam ändre der Mensch selbst die bestimmte Ge-
O, gedenke denn auch, wie aus dem Keim der Bekannt-
  schaft
Nach und nach in uns holde Gewohnheit entspross,
Freundschaft sich mit Macht in unserm Innern ent-
  hüllte,
  Und wie Amor zuletzt Blüthen und Früchte gezeugt.
Denke, wie mannigfach bald die, bald jene Gestalten,
  Still entfaltend, Natur unsern Gefühlen geliehn!
Freue dich auch des heutigen Tags! Die heilige Liebe
  Strebt zu der höchsten Frucht gleicher Gessinungen
  auf,
Gleicher Ansicht der Dinge, damit in harmonischem
  Anschaun
  Sich verbinde das Paar, finde die höhere Welt.

METAMORPHOSIS of PLANTS.

Thee perplexes, beloved, the thousandfold intermixture
  of this flowery throng, around in the garden.
Manynames hearest thou, and ever one chases the other,
  with barbarian sound, out of the listener's ear.

All the forms are resembling, and no one is *like* to
    another;
  and thus does the chorus point to a mysterious law,
a holy riddle.   Oh, could I to thee, lovely friend,
  at once happily impart the solving word!
Mark now the progress—how by degrees the plant
  step-wise led up, forms itself to blossom and to fruit.
Out of the seed it unfolds itself, soon as the earth
  softly lets it forth into life, out of her fructifying lap;
and to the attraction of light, the holy, the eternally-
    moving
  commends the tenderest structure of budding leaves.
Simple slept in the seed the (germinating) power; an
    incipient foretype
lay enfolded within itself, compressed within the husk,
root, and leaf, and bud; only half formed and colour-
    less;
  thus does the dry kernel protect the silent life;
it shoots, striving upwards, trusting itself to the gentle
    moisture,
  and soon rears itself out of surrounding night.
But simple remains the form in its earliest appearance,
  and thus, even among plants, is infancy distinguished.
Quickly, then, a successive impulse, arising, repeats
  joint upon joint, built up; ever the primitive type.
Not indeed always the same; for manifold shoots forth,
  fashioned out, as thou seest, leaf succeeding to leaf;
more outspread, more indented, more distinct in points
    and in parts,

which formerly slept scarce shaped, in the lowermost
organ.

And so attains it, at first, its highest destined completion,
which, in many a tribe, awakens thy mind to amaze-
ment.

Variously ribbed and jagged, on the juicy exuberant
surface

free and infinite seems the impulse which causes the
growth.

But now, Nature, with powerful hand, suddenly checks
the formation,

and gently diverts it towards a higher perfection.

In slenderer streams now leads she the sap, the vessels
she narrows,

and quickly the structure betrays the more delicate
workings.

The vigorous outshooting force of the branches softly
relaxes,

and the frame of the stem takes a more perfect con-
sistence.

Leafless, however, and rapid, up darts the slenderer
flower-stalk,

and a wonderful picture attracts the observer's eye.

Round in a circle now range themselves, counted or
countless,

the lesser leaves, each next to one like it.

The sheltering calix, pressed round a centre, unfolds,
and, to finish the work, lets forth the gay coloured
crown.

And now Nature blooms, in her highest fullest magnificence,
and limb on limb she displays, upreared in beautiful
series.
Ever thy wonder is new, as, on the flower-stalk, the flower
waves above the slender framework of changing leaves.
But this glorious show is the herald of new operations ;
yes, the gay coloured leaf feels the all-powerful hand.
Quickly now it shrinks up ; the most delicate forms
then on each side strive forward, towards their destined union.
Fondly stand they together, the affianced beautiful
couples,
or in numbers around the holy altar are ranged.
Hymen hovers near, and exquisite odours
stream around, with sweet all-quickening power.
Now, compacted together, swell countless distinct germs
of the swelling fruit, in the lap of the bountiful mother.
And here Nature closes the ring of her eternal powers ;
but a new one instantly enlinks itself on the former,
that the chain may be lengthened out through all time,
and that the Whole may have life, as well as each
several Being.
And now, oh beloved, turn thine eye on the many-hued
throng
which no longer moves in perplexing confusion before thee.
Every plant now proclaims to thee immutable laws ;
every flower now speaks clearer and clearer to thee.

But if here thou decipher'st the sacred letters of the
  Goddess,
  every where wilt thou see them, though in differing
  forms.
Creeping may loiter the grub, swift fly the butterfly,
  man, with plastic powers, may change his determined
  form.
Oh bethink thee then, too, how, out of the germ of acquaintance,
  by little and little in us the affectionate usage* arose;
how, in our inmost hearts, friendship then strongly
  revealed itself,
  and how love, at last, brought us his flowers and his
  fruit.
Think, how manifold-wise, now this, now the other form,
  silently unfolding, Nature has lent to our feelings!
Rejoice in the day that is! holy Love strives
  after the loftiest fruit of equal, resembling minds,
of similar views of things—whereby in harmonious insight
  those who love may be one—may find the Higher
  World.

It appears that he pursued this study during his
travels in Italy. In a letter dated Naples, 25th
March, 1786, I find the following:—" I beg you

* *Gewohnheit,* consuetudo. *Familiarity* comes the
nearest to it, but this, like so many of our words, is
vulgarized.

to tell Herder that I have almost finished my Archetypal Plant (*Urpflanz*), only I am afraid nobody will choose to recognize in it the actual vegetable world. My famous Theory of Cotyledons is so sublimated that it would be a hard matter to push it further."

In May of the same year, in a letter to Herder, he says, "I must moreover tell you in confidence, that I am very near the whole secret of the generation and organization of plants, and that it is the simplest thing that can be imagined. Under this sky one may make the most beautiful observations. The main point—where the germ really lodges—I have discovered beyond all doubt; all the rest I have a general view of, only some points must be more distinctly made out. The Archetypal Plant (*Urpflanz*) will be the strangest creature in the world, which Nature herself shall envy me. With this model, and the key to it, one may then invent plants *ad infinitum*, which *must* be consistent; *i. e.* which, if they do not exist, yet might exist, and are not mere picturesque shows and shadows, but have an inward truth and necessity. The same law will be applicable to all animated bodies."

In April, 1788 (*Zweyter Aufenthalt in Rom,*) he writes, " The laws of the organization of plants which I had detected in Sicily, busied me, in the midst of all these other pursuits, as favourite studies do which take hold in our minds, and seem to lie within our reach. I visited the botanic garden, and collected many curious plants on which to prosecute my observations."

1798.—" I wrote notes on Diderot's Essay on Colours, rather humourous than scientific. * *
* * * * * * * * * * * * *
In what order and division the history of the Theory of Colours should be given, was thought out chronologically (*epochen-weise*), and the several writers on the subject studied : the theory itself, too, was maturely weighed, and discussed with Schiller. He it was who resolved the doubt which had long hindered me—what was the cause of that strange uncertainty of vision from which some men confound colours. He inferred from it, that they see some colours and do not see others, and at length concluded that they entirely want the perception of blue. A young man of the name of Gildemeister, who was then a student at Jena, had this defect, and very kindly offered himself for all sort of experiments, which at length confirmed us in this result."

1800.—" The investigation of nature went on its quiet course. * * * * * * * * *

The main divisions of the *Farbenlehre*, under the three great heads, the Didactic, the Polemic, and the Historic, now first became clear and distinct to my mind.

" To make myself perfect in Jussieu's System of Botany, I arranged the plates of several botanical works in that order. I thence derived a perception (*Anschauung*) of the individual forms, and a general view of the whole, which I could have obtained by no other means."

1801.—Being ill, he says, he was obliged to work with moderation. " I therefore turned myself to the translation of Theophrastus's little book on colours, which I had long had in my mind."

1802.—On his visit to Halle, he says, " With Loder, many anatomical problems formerly observed were discussed. With Himly, a great deal concerning subjective vision, and the appearance of colours. We often lost ourselves so deeply in our subject, that we wandered over hill and dale till far into the night."

1806.—" Cotta's observations on the growth of plants, with specimens of sections of various woods, were a very welcome present. These observations stimulated me to renew those which I had had such a lingering after for so many years, and were the main cause that I resolved to addict myself anew to Morphology, and to print the *Metamorphose der Pflanzen*, and something appended to it.

" The preliminary labours to the *Farbenlehre*, with which I had been occupied during twelve consecutive years, were advanced so far, that the parts began to assume a certain coherence, and the whole promised soon to acquire consistency. What I, after my fashion, could and would do, as to physiological colours, was done. The beginning of the historical part likewise lay ready, and the printing of the first and second parts might therefore be begun. I now turned to the pathological colours, and, with relation to the historical part, investigated what Pliny had said of colours. While the several parts thus went forward, a scheme of the whole science was worked out.

" The physical colours now required arrangement, and my whole attention. The observation of their media, and conditions of appearance, put the whole powers of my mind in requisition. Here I was compelled to express my long-confirmed conviction, that, as we see all colours only through media, and on media, the doctrine of Opakes (*Trüben*) as the purest and most delicate material, was the beginning whence the whole scale of colours must unfold itself.

" Persuaded that in what lay behind me within

the circle of physiological colours, this must of necessity come to light without any efforts of mine, I went forwards, and arranged all I had gone through with myself or with others, on refraction. For this was truly the abode of that enchanted princess, who in her seven-coloured garment deceives the world. Here lay the grim sophistical dragon, the terror of all who resolved to undertake the adventure of a combat with this error. The importance of this point, and of the chapter thereto belonging, was great. I sought to do justice to it by copious investigation, and do not fear having to reproach myself with the neglect of anything. That when colours appear by refraction, some figure, outline, or boundary line must be displaced, was established. How, in subjective experiments, black and white objects of all sorts, when looked at through the prism, retain their outlines; how the same is the case with regard to gray objects of all shades, and to the bright colours of every variety and shade, according to the greater or less degree of refraction; all this was rigidly examined, and I am convinced that the teacher who shall put all the phenomena to the test of experiment, will find nothing wanting either in the matter or the statement.

"The catoptrical and paroptical colours followed

next ; and it was in the attempt to observe them that it appeared, that reflection in a mirror produced colours only when the reflecting body was scratched, cracked, or used in threads or strips. In the experiments on the paroptical colours I was led to deny the inclination (curvature?), and to deduce the coloured stripes from double lights. That each of the edges of the sun throws a distinct shadow of its own, was exhibited in a very striking manner by an annular solar eclipse.

" The sensual and moral effect of colours was then examined, and, in the historical department, Gauthier's *Chroagénésie* was read. We had come to the thirteenth sheet of the first part, when, on the 14th of October, the most dreadful calamity fell upon us, and threatened irretrievably to destroy the papers, which were hastily put together for flight.

" Happily, we soon recovered ourselves, and were able to engage in new pursuits, and to resume this, and to go on in our daily work with calm activity.

" Now, above all, were the necessary tables constructed. A continued correspondence with the kind and excellent Runge gave us opportunity to annex his letters at the end of the *Farbenlehre*. Seebeck's series of experiments also came very opportunely to hand. With lightened breast we thanked the Muses for such manifest favour ; but scarcely had we taken breath, when we found ourselves compelled to enter upon the odious polemical part of the affair, and to bring our labours on Newton's Optics, as well as the examination of his experiments and the inductions from them, into a narrow compass, and thus to a termination. The introduction to the polemical part began with the year."

1807.—" The long-prepared tables for the *Farbenlehre* were gradually drawn out fair, with great pains and accuracy, and engraved, while the printing of the text went on, and was finished in the end of January. Now, I could turn with more freedom to the polemical part. As Newton had come at an inconclusive result by connecting different instruments and contrivances, the phenomena which arise when prisms and lenses operate on each other were investigated, and the Newtonian experiments accurately examined, one after the other. The beginning of the polemical part was thus ready for press. The historical was kept steadily in view. Nuguet on colours, in the *Journal de Trévoux,* was most welcome. I went back, too, to the middle ages ; Roger Bacon was taken up again, and, as a preparatory work, I wrote the Scheme of the Fifteenth Century.

" Friend Meyer* studied the colouring of the ancients, and began an essay upon it. The merits of these never enough to be valued fathers of art, were faithfully represented in all their purity and nature. An introduction to the *Farbenlehre*, and a preface, were written ; a zealous friend also attempted a translation into French, the pages of which, still in my possession, recal to me the most delightful hours. Meanwhile, the polemical part was continued, and the printed sheets of both parts corrected. At the end of the year, there were thirty sheets of the first, and five of the second part, in my hands.

" When we have been long occupied with a subject, and it is become so familiar to us and so much our own that it floats before our minds on every occasion, we come to use it by way of comparison or illustration, both in jest and in earnest ; this I experienced, in some pleasant instances, with cheerful friends, in our literary intercommunications.

" The polemical, as well as the historical part of the Theory of Colours goes on slowly, but regularly. Of historical studies, Roger Bacon, Aquilouius, and Boyle, are the chief remaining. At the end of the year, the first part is nearly finished.

* See Note 8.

1809.—" At Jena, I worked upon the History of the Theory of Colours ; went over the 15th and 16th centuries, and wrote the history of my own chromatic conversion and continued researches. I laid this work by in May, and did not resume it till the end of the year, when Runge's *Farben-kugel* (colour-sphere?) set my chromatic observations in motion again. I then brought the history down to the 18th century, and the printing of the second part went on uninterruptedly. My attention was next directed to the controversy with Newton.

1810.—" A remarkable year, diversified by activity, enjoyment, and acquisition. The whole is so superabundant, that I feel myself in perplexity how to arrange the parts in due order.

" Before all things, however, science deserves mention. In this respect, the beginning of the year was tiresome enough ; I had got so far with the printing of the *Farbenlehre*, that the completion of it before Easter seemed not impossible. I finished the polemical part, as well as the history of the 18th century; the tables, engraved after my careful drawings, were coloured ; the recapitulation of the whole concluded, and the departure of the last sheet for the printing-office was seen with delight.

" This took place just eighteen years after the first perception of a long-cherished error, after a course of unwearied labours ; and after the discovery, at length, of the point around which all must congregate. The burthen I had hitherto borne was so great, that I looked upon the 16th of May, on which I seated myself in the carriage on my way to Bohemia, as a happy day of liberation.

" As to the effect, I troubled myself little ; and I did well. For such a perfect want of sympathy, and repulsive unfriendliness, however, I was not prepared. I say nothing about it, and rather prefer to mention how much I was indebted, in this and in all my other scientific and literary labours, to Dr. F. W. Riemer, many years companion of my house, my travels, and my studies.

" But as, when one is once accustomed to toil and trouble, one is ever ready and willing to take up fresh burthens ; on looking over the scheme of the *Farbenlehre,* the kindred idea suggested itself whether the science of sounds might not be treated in a similar manner ; and gave birth to a table, in which Subject, Object, and Medium were arranged in three columns.

" And as none of our mental powers can easily deviate from the track which we have once fallen into, be it the true or the false one, this same mode of presenting a thing to the mind was applied to the whole of physics : the Subject, with full consideration of its organs of apprehension and perception; the Object, as something perceptible; the Phenomenon (*Erscheinung*—appearance), repeated and varied by experiment, in the centre; whence a completely new mode of investigation was devised.

" Experiment, as proof of any subjective opinion, was rejected. There exist what have long been called questions in nature. And as all discovery may be regarded as a wise answer to a prudent question*, one may at every step convince oneself whether or not one is on the right road, when one sees everywhere, whether in the Particular or the Universal, nothing but gain on one's side."

1812.—" Dr. Seebeck, following his chromatic investigations with his usual industry, occupied himself with the second Newtonian experiment, which I had only touched upon as much as was absolutely necessary in the polemical part of my work. He worked at it in my presence, and arrived at some important results; for that theory, as soon as you proceed from the use of the prism

---

* Lord Bacon says, " A prudent questioning is a kind of half knowledge."—*Transl.*

to that of lenses, becomes entangled in inextricable difficulties.

1814.—" In the *Farbenlehre* something was progressively done. The entoptic colours remain a constant object of attention. The meeting with Dr. Seebeck, at Frankfurt, was a great advantage; for, independent of his general and comprehensive knowledge, he had gone to the bottom of the theory of the double spar, and knew how to bring before the eyes of enquirers the relation of the axes of such refracting bodies.

" The theory of sounds was compared with that of colours. Professor Voigt pursued his observations, particularly on the colours of organic bodies; and over all my researches into natural history, floated Howard's Theory of Clouds."

1816.—" Professor Pfaff sent me his attack on my *Farbenlehre*, according to the uncivil intrusiveness in fashion among German authors. I laid it aside till some future day, when my own mind may be fully made up. To follow one's own way must ever be the safest plan; for this always has the peculiar advantage of always leading us back from all our errors to ourselves.

" Dr. Schopenhauer came to my side, as a friend and well-wisher. We discussed many things, and were generally agreed. * * * * * * *

Experiments on colours, with vegetable extracts, served repeatedly to show the great consistency (consequentiality) of the theory of colours."

1817.—" I worked with great zeal at the second part of the Morphology, and made historical observations on the influence of the Kantian doctrines on my studies. * * * * * * * *

" My chromatic pursuits occupied me in silence. I endeavoured to make myself acquainted with what had been done on the subject in England, France, and Germany. I studied four English authors of distinguished reputation, and sought to make their works, and ways of thinking, clear and distinct to my own mind; these were Bancroft, Sowerby, Reid, and Brewster. On the one side I remarked, with pleasure, that they, by pure observation of phenomena, had approached the course indicated by nature, and, indeed, had sometimes touched it; on the other I saw, with regret, that they could not entirely free themselves from the dominion of the old error,—that colour is contained in light; that they made use of the established terminology; and thence fell into the greatest confusion and intricacy. Brewster especially, too, seemed to think that the thing was advanced by an endless series of experiments; whereas, numerous and accurate experiments are only the preliminary labours of the true investigator of nature, to enable him to arrive, at length, at a result freed from all subordinate or collateral matters.

" The most offensive thing to me, however, that ever came under my notice, was Biot's chapter on the entoptic colours, called by him the Polarization of light. By taking a false analogy—that of a magnetic needle—he had distorted light into two poles, and thus (no less than had formerly been done) had sought to explain colours by differentializing the Unchangeable and Untouchable. Then, to bolster up a false dogma with proofs, the whole armoury of mathematics was put in requisition, so that nature wholly and utterly vanished from both the outward and inward sense. I could only look upon the whole business as a pathological *case*; it was as if a splinter had been forced into some organized body, and an unskilful surgeon, instead of instantly extracting it, had bestowed his whole care upon the swelling, and had endeavoured to soothe and reduce that, while the cause of the evil was internally working incurable mischief.

" And thus it was quite dreadful to me, when an academical teacher, with incredible coolness and confidence, spread forth the most inconclusive, inapplicable apparatus before eminent and discriminating persons; and after looking and re-looking, blinking with one eye and then with the other, nobody knew either what he had seen, or what he ought to see. I had risen and left the room at the first display, and heard the result of these *demonstrations* at my return without the least surprise. The audience had the good fortune to learn, too, on this occasion, by the example of two billiard balls, that the globules of light, when they come in contact with glass, at the poles, go through and through; but when they come upon it at the equator, are sent back again with a flea in their ear.

" Meanwhile, the entoptic experiments multiplied to infinity, since I had at last to discover the simple atmospheric origin. * * * * *
* * * * * * * * * * * * * *

" Leonardo da Vinci's essay on the causes of the blueness of distant mountains, and other objects, gave me renewed pleasure. He hit upon the right, because he understood nature from immediate inspection, and reflected on the appearances themselves, with the perspicacity of a true Artist. I had also the sympathy of some observing and thinking men. Staatsrath Schultz, of Berlin, sent me his second paper on physiological colours, where I saw my leading idea brought into life and action. Nor was I less satisfied with Professor Hegel's approbation. Since Schiller's death, I had silently withdrawn myself from all philosophy, and only sought to bring that Method (*Methodik*) which was native to me, to greater certainty and readiness, by the application of it to Nature, Art, and Life. It must, therefore, be very gratifying to me to see and reflect how what I had submitted, after *my* fashion, was received and handled by a philosopher, according to *his* kind of knowledge. And here it was perfectly granted me, to consider the mysterious, clear Light as the highest energy; eternal, sole, and indivisible."

1818.—" At the same time, the chapter of en-toptic colours was in the order of the day. Brewster's experiments for communicating to glass the regular appearance of colours by reflection, by means of pressure, which had been usually produced by means of heat, succeeded perfectly; and I, for my part, persuaded of the co-operation of the Techno-mechanic with the Dynamo-ideal, had Seebeck's cross embroidered like damask, and could now see it in whatever light I chose, clear or dim, on an uniform surface."

1820.—" The entoptic colours gave me fresh zeal for working at the theory of colours. I had concluded my essay, with great care, in the August of this year, and sent it to press. The order I had followed in my *Farbenlehre* was observed here also. The entoptic apparatus was further simplified. Laminæ of mica and gypsum were used in experiments, and their effects carefully compared. I had the good luck to go through this matter, once more, with Staatsrath Schultz, and immediately set myself upon various paralipomena of the theory of colours.

" Purkinje on Vision was taken in hand, and the adversaries of my doctrines arranged chronologically. My attention was directed, by some of my friends, to the *Nouvelle Chroagénésie, par le Prince,* which might be regarded as the effect and corroboration of my *Farbenlehre.* On examination, however, I found an important difference. The author had come upon the track of Newton's error, in the same way that I had ; but he advanced neither himself nor others, since he, like Dr. Reid, wanted to establish something equally untenable in the place of it. This gave me occasion to remark, once more, how a man who has been struck and enlightened by a ray of light, can fall back again so quickly into the darkness of his *individuum,* in which he then tries to grope his way by the miserable help of a farthing rushlight.

" A great many observations on the march of

science—on its advance, retardation, nay, even re-trogradation, were made. The mutual relation of all physical phenomena, ever coming more to light, yet still veiled in mystery, was modestly examined into; till, all at once, the discovery of the relation between galvanism and magnetism, by Professor Oerstadt, burst upon us with an almost dazzling light. On the other hand, I regarded with horror an instance of the most terrible *obscurantism*, in studying more nearly Biot's works on the polarization of light. One really grows ill over such an attempt. Such theories, proofs, and details, are real Nekroses, against which the most vigorous organization cannot stand."

1821.—" I now turn to the natural sciences; and must remark, in the first place, that Purkinje's work on subjective Sight peculiarly excited me. I wrote notes, and, with the view of making use of it in my essays, had the tables which are annexed copied. As the whole theory of colours rests on a precise idea of Opakes (*Trüben*)—since it is by them that we arrive at the perception of the primitive phenomenon—and since, by a careful and able development of it, we find the whole visible world made clear to us, it was worth while to look around, how various nations had expressed themselves on this subject; from what point they set out, and how they made use of nearer or more remote, ruder or more delicate, analogies. I tried to get possession of some Vienna drinking glasses, on which an opake enamel, or glazing, exhibited the phenomenon more beautifully than I had seen it in any other way.

" Much chromatic matter was looked out of former papers, for my fourth number. Bernardinus Telesius was studied generally, and particularly the part on colours. Seebeck's lecture on the warmth of prismatic figures of the sun (?) (*Sonnenbilde*) was most welcome ; and my own earlier observations on these remarkable facts were revealed. Hofmechanicus Körner busied himself with an attempt to make flint glass, and erected an instrument in his workshop, for the so-called polarization experiments, on the French plan. The results were, as I had long ago convinced myself they would be, slender enough. It was singular, that, just at the same time, a feud broke out between Biot and Arago, by which the nullity of this theory was made sufficiently evident to all men of science.

" In my chromatic studies, I had a great acquisition ; for, at length, there appeared a hope that a younger man would take upon himself the duty of carrying and fighting through this important matter. Herr von Henning visited me, and brought admirably prepared entoptic glasses and black mirrors, which, combined, bring before the eye all the most important phenomena, with little trouble or preparation. Our conversation was easy; he had gone thoroughly into the subject; and some questions on which he was still in doubt, I could answer. He told me how he had treated it in his lectures, the introduction to which he had already communicated to me. We interchanged our views and experiments; I gave him an old essay of mine on prisms in connection with lenses, which had hitherto been employed to a false end; and he, in return, urged me to put my chromatic papers into more perfect and available order. This all happened in autumn, and gave me no little tranquillity.

" An entoptic apparatus was fitted up, and sent to Berlin; the simple entoptic glasses, with black glass mirrors, had put us upon a new course, had increased our discoveries, enlarged our views, and given occasion to observe the entoptic quality of melting ice."

I have, I believe, picked out nearly every sentence relating to these two works of Goethe's, particularly the *Farbenlehre*, from his *Tag-und-*

Jahres Hefte ; a little book, which seems to me singularly interesting, instructive, and characteristic, and which I should feel myself most usefully employed in translating, if I had any expectation that the public would judge it as I do. The calm observation, the indulgent judgement, the unwearied industry, the wonderful many-sidedness, the resolution to use and to enjoy life to the utmost, which are evident in every page of these annals of his mind and works, afford a most beautiful study, rich in lessons of utility and happiness.

The book is full of entertaining matter ; and it may appear strange that I have selected just the part which is least interesting to myself—to which, in my total ignorance of physical science, I could least do justice, and which will least amuse the " general reader." But I thought *this* view of the mental activity of the author of Werther, Iphigenia, and Faust, quite worth the notice of every one who desires to understand Goethe. Allowance must be made for defects of translation, on a subject of which I know nothing. The *Tag-und-Jahres Hefte* is a sort of *Biographia Literaria* ; poetry, painting, music,—geology, and other physical sciences,—pass in review before the author, and are pursued with the ardour and perseverance of which I have given one example.

The observations on cotemporary literature, persons, and events are most amusing and instructive. The description of Madame de Stael's visit to Weimar, of his own visit to Carlsbad, may be mentioned as peculiarly entertaining. The remarks on the characters of others are full of acuteness, yet always calm, and generally leaning to the favourable side. The insight afforded into his own, is wonderfully interesting; sometimes designed, sometimes unconscious; and, to conclude all, the picture of the life of a man of letters, in one of the " despotic" states of Germany, is fitted to excite some reflections not altogether favourable to " popular institutions," in those who live in a country where government and people are too much occupied in scrambling for supremacy, to care about arts or letters.

It will be observed that, in recording his proceedings, Goethe frequently uses either the first person plural, or the impersonal form of speech. In the original this is much more frequent than I found it expedient to adopt. I have retained it where I could, without ambiguity or awkwardness, as I endeavour to do whatever is characteristic in his style.

Some remarks on the two works which form the subject of this Note will be found in an interesting article on Goethe, which has lately appeared in the *Bibliothèque Universelle* of Geneva, and of which I have

NOTE 5.

Johann Heinrich Voss was born in 1751, in a village of Mecklenburg, where his father was a farmer. He afterwards removed to Penzlin, where Johann was educated till his fourteenth year. As a child, he was remarkable for strength of memory, universal curiosity, and an enthusiastic tendency to self-observation. He was of a delicate constitution, and his amusements were the Bible, and popular tales and ballads. In 1766, he went to school in New Brandenburg, and, having already taught himself some Greek and Hebrew, entered the highest class. Greek being neglected, Voss secretly formed a class of twelve of the head boys, who met to repair this defect by their private exertions. Fines were exacted for negligence, and these went to the purchase of a common stock of German classics. Here he already began to write verses. His father's circumstances, however, growing more and more straitened, young Voss entered the family of a country gentleman,

been glad to avail myself in a later part of my work. It is said to be written by a young Genevese, who is now tutor to the young Princes of Weimar.

near Penzlin, as private tutor. After teaching five or six hours a day, his recreations were the study of the ancient languages, music, and solitary walks in the neighbouring wood, where he used to declaim aloud, passages from Horace, Rammler, and other poets ; and where he made his translation of Hesiod's Theogony. He became acquainted with Brückner and Boie, by the latter of whom he was induced to go to Göttingen, where Boie had obtained for him commons (*freitisch*) for two years, and hoped to get him private pupils and free instruction (*freies collegium*). Here he became one of that band of distinguished youths, at the head of which were Boie and Bürger. Voss determined to enter the church ; and the first courses he attended were, consequently, logic, history, and dogmatic theology (*die Dogmatik*), and the Psalms. He, however, abandoned theology, and devoted himself exclusively to Greek and Latin literature. He now entered Heyne's philological seminary ; besides which, he attended his lectures on the last books of the Iliad, and some private lectures, especially on Pindar. He, however, quarrelled with Heyne, and quitted Göttingen. He translated Blackwell's work on Homer ; and in 1775 retired to Wandsbeck, to conduct the Göttingen *Musen-Almanack*, in the quiet of the country. In 1778, through the interest of Büsch, he became rector* at Otterndorf in Hadeln, where he became acquainted with another remarkable instance of vigorous self-education, Carsten Niebuhr, the traveller, father of the illustrious and lamented historian†. Here he published his translation of the Odyssey. Incessant marsh fever drove him from Otterndorf, and he went as rector to Eutin. In 1793 he published his Iliad and Odyssey; and in 1801 his beautiful poem, *Luise*. We pass over the mention of numerous less celebrated works. In 1805, the Grand Duke of Baden invited him to Heidelberg, to assist in restoring the University. Here he died, on the 30th of March, 1826, strengthened and tranquillized by domestic patriarchal repose, and the consciousness of having ever willed the Good, the True, the Right. In reviewing his life, it is impossible to deny that, through his whole career, as poet and philologist, as teacher and friend, he toiled, nay, combated, for truth and justice, for the universal ennobling of his species: we find, in him, a thorough German character, amiable in social intercourse, patriarchal, simple, and friendly; his faults were, vanity, pertinacity of opinion, and

* Not a clerical office.
† See Carsten Niebuhr's Life, by his son.

contentiousness. As philologist, he had a most intimate acquaintance with the antients, both with their lives and language, and his services to the German language and metre are beyond all praise. As translator of the poets of antiquity, he unquestionably holds the highest place; and it is delightful to observe with what intense perseverance, with what conscientious strictness, with what metrical art, he strove after pre-excellence in this line. The Homer, and the Eclogues of Virgil, are his best works. Horace, Aristophanes, and Shakspeare, are far less successful. Some of his earlier songs and idyls are very beautiful. Of the latter, the *Luise* is incomparably the most celebrated, and is a wonderful adaptation of the tone of Theocritus, and sometimes of Homer, to genuine German domestic life.

An account of Voss will be found in Mr. William Taylor's Survey of German Poetry, vol. ii. I have, however, extracted the foregoing from the Conversations Lexicon, as it appeared necessary to the understanding of the beautiful exposition of the life and works of a Poet which follows. This is to be found in the volume of Goethe's *Recensionen*. I have little fear of presenting my readers with what is already familiar to them, for I have met with accomplished Germans, admirers of Goethe, who had never seen it, and who were as much struck as I had been by its beauty. A volume of the best specimens of German criticism would be a valuable addition to English literature. In them is kept in view the proper end and province of criticism—the *instruction* of the author and o the public. The following, however, is rather an analysis of the character of the Poet than of the Poems.

REVIEW of VOSS'S POEMS: extracted from Vol. xxxiii. of Goethe's Works, last edition, 1830. *Lyrical Poems of Johann Heinrich Voss.* 1802. *First Volume, Odes and Elegies, &c.*

" Looking at the index of poems prefixed to each volume, we find the odes and elegies of the first volume, as well as the odes and songs of the three following, and all the other small poems, arranged according to the date of their composition.

" Such a compilation and mode of arrangement generally, and in this case particularly, bespeaks a tranquil, consistent, gradually-pursued progress in mental culture, and gives us a presentiment, that, in this collection, more clearly perhaps than in any other, the life, the walk, and conversation of the poet are pictured out.

" Every author, in some degree, pourtrays himself in his works, even be it against his will. In this case, he is present to us, and designedly; nay, with a friendly alacrity, sets before us his inward and outward modes of thinking and feeling; and disdains not to give us confidential explanations of circumstances, thoughts, views, and expressions, by means of appended notes.

" And now, encouraged by so friendly an invitation, we draw nearer to him; we seek him by himself; we attach ourselves to him, and promise ourselves rich enjoyment, and manifold instruction and improvement.

" In a level northern landscape, we find him, rejoicing in his existence, in a latitude in which the antients hardly expected to find a living thing.

" And truly, Winter there manifests his whole might and sovereignty. Storm-borne from the Pole, he covers the wood with hoar frost, the streams with ice;—a drifting whirlwind eddies around the high gables, while the poet rejoices in the shelter and comfort of his home, and cheerily bids defiance to the raging elements. Furred and frost-covered friends arrive, and are heartily welcomed under the protecting roof; and soon they form a cordial, confiding circle, enliven the household meal by the clang of glasses, the joyous song, and thus create for themselves a moral summer.

" We then find him abroad, and braving the inclemencies of the wintry heavens. When the axle-tree creaks heavily under the load of fire-wood—when even the footsteps of the wanderer ring along the ground—we see him now walking briskly through the snow to the distant dwelling of a friend; now joining a sledge-party, gliding, with tinkling bells, over the boundless plain. At length a cheerful inn receives the half-frozen tra-vellers; a bright flickering fire greets them as they crowd around the chimney; dance, choral song, and many a warm viand, are reviving and grateful to youth and age. But when the snow melts under the returning sun, when the warmed earth frees itself somewhat from its thick cover-ing, the poet hastens with his friends into the free air, to refresh himself with the first living breath of the new year, and to seek the earliest flowers. The bright golden clover is gathered, bound into bunches, and brought home in triumph, where this herald of the future beauty and bounty of the year is destined to crown a family festival of Hope.

" And when Spring herself advances, no more is heard of roof and hearth; the poet is always abroad, wandering on the soft pathways, around his peaceful lake. Every bush unfolds itself with an individual character, every blossom bursts with an individual life, in his presence. As in a fully worked-out picture, we see, in the sun-light around him, grass and herb, as distinctly as oak and beech-tree; and on the margin of the still waters there is wanting neither the reed nor any succulent plant.

" Here his companions are not those transforming fantasies, by whose impatient power the rock fashions itself into the divine maiden, the tree puts off its branches and appears to allure the hunter with its soft, lovely arms. Rather wanders the poet solitary, like a priest of nature; touches each plant, each bush, with gentle hand; and hallows them members of a loving, barmonious family.

" Around him, like a dweller in Eden, sport harmless, fearless creatures—the lamb on the meadows, the roe in the forest. Around him, assemble the whole choir of birds, and drown the busy hum of day with their varied accents.

" Then, at evening, towards night, when the moon climbs the heaven in serene splendour, and sends her flickering image curling to his feet on the surface of the lightly ruffled waters ; when the boat rocks softly, and the oar gives its measured cadence, and every stroke calls up sparkles of reflected light; when the nightingale pours forth her divine song from the shore, and softens every heart; then do affection and passion manifest themselves in happy tenderness; from the first touch of a sympathy awakened by the Highest himself, to that quiet, graceful, timid desire, which flourishes within the narrow enclosure of domestic life. A heaving breast, an ardent glance, a pressure of the hand, a stolen kiss, give life to his song. But it is ever the affianced lover that is emboldened; it is ever the betrothed bride that yields; and thus does all that is ventured, and all that is granted, bend to a lawful standard; though, within that limit, he permits himself much freedom.

"Soon, however, he leads us again under the free heavens; into the green; to bower and bush; and there is he most cheerfully, cordially, and fondly at home.

"The Summer has come again; a genial warmth breathes through the poet's song. Thunders roll; clouds drop showers; rainbows appear; lightnings gleam; and a blessed coolness overspreads the plain. Every thing ripens; the poet overlooks none of the varied harvests; he hallows all by his presence.

"And here is the place to remark what an influence our poets might exercise on the civilization of our German people—in some places, perhaps, have exercised.

" His poems on the various incidents of rural life, indeed, do represent rather the reflections of a refined intellect than the feelings of the common people; but if we could picture to ourselves that a harper were present at the hay, corn, and potatoe harvests,—if we recollected how he might make the men whom he gathered around him observant of that which recurs to them as ordinary and familiar; if, by his manner of regarding it, by his poetical expression, he elevated the Common, and heightened the enjoyment of every gift of God and nature by his dignified representation of it, we may truly say he would be a real benefactor to his country. For the first stage of a true enlightenment is, that man should reflect upon his condition and circumstances, and be brought to regard them in the most agreeable light. Let the song of the potatoe be sung in the field, where the wondrous mode of increase, which calls even the man of science to high and curious meditation, after the long and silent working and interweaving of vegetable powers, comes to view, and a quite unintelligible blessing springs out of the earth; and then first will be felt the merit of this and similar poems, in which the poet essays to awaken the rude, reckless, unobservant man, who takes every thing for granted, to an attentive observation of the high wonders of all-nourishing Nature, by which he is constantly surrounded.

" But scarcely are all these bounties brought under man's notice, when Autumn glides in, and our poet takes an affecting leave of nature, decaying, at least in outward appearance. Yet he abandons not his beloved vegetation wholly to the unkind winter. The elegant vase receives many a plant, many a bulb, wherewith to create a mimic summer in the home seclusion of winter, and, even at that season, to leave no festival without its flowers and wreaths. Care is taken that even the household birds belonging to the family should not want a green, fresh roof to their bowery cage.

" Now is the loveliest time for short rambles,— for friendly converse in the chilly evening. Every domestic feeling becomes active; longings for social pleasures increase; the want of music is more sensibly felt; and now, even the sick man willingly joins the friendly circle, and a departing friend seems to clothe himself in the colours of the departing year.

" For, as certainly as spring will return after the lapse of winter, so certainly will friends, lovers, kindred, meet again; they will meet again in the presence of the all-loving Father; and then first will they form a Whole with each other, and with every thing good, after which they sought and strove in vain in this piece-meal world. And thus does the felicity of the poet, even here, rest on the persuasion that all have to rejoice in the care of a wise God, whose power extends unto all, and whose light lightens upon all. Thus does the adoration of such a Being create in the poet the highest clearness and reasonableness; and, at the same time, an assurance that the thoughts, the words, with which he comprehends and describes infinite qualities, are not empty dreams and sounds; and thence arises a rapturous feeling of his own and others' happiness, in which every thing conflicting, peculiar, discordant, is resolved and dissipated.

" Thus far we have seen the gentle, serene, collected nature of our poet, in peace with himself, with God, and with the world; but may not even this self-dependence, from whose inner circles expands so cheerful an existence, be frequently troubled, perplexed, and excited to passionate emotion from without? These questions, also, may be fully answered from the poems before us.

" The conviction of having, by his own proper strength and steadfast will, raised himself out of cramping circumstances, and educated himself out of himself; of owing his merits to himself alone; of being able to gain and to increase these advantages solely by an unfettered aspiration of the mind, enhances the natural feeling of independence, which, constantly heightened by abstraction from the world, must receive many a check, many a wound, from the inevitable intercourses of life.

" When, therefore, the poet is compelled to remark that so many members of the higher classes neglect the great privileges and invaluable facilities their birth affords them, and that ill-breeding; coarseness, and want of cultivation prevail among them, he cannot pardon such disgraceful recklessness. And if, moreover, they look down upon true merit with all the arrogance of ignorance and stupidity, he draws back in disgust, and secludes himself even from the cheerful repast and the convivial circle, where frank humanity and kindness stream from heart to heart, and common enjoyment ought to knit the most delightful bond of union.

" With holy, solemn earnestness, he contrasts true merit with false; now chastises exclusive prejudice and ignorance with ridicule, now seeks to correct error by love.

" But where the advantages of birth are enhanced

by intrinsic worth, he greets them with sincere respect, and wins to himself the most valuable friends.

" He takes a transient part in that poetical enthusiasm for freedom which was awakened and maintained in Germany during the enjoyment of a ten years' peace. Many a well-disposed youth, who carried the feeling of academic independence into life and art, found, in the restraints of civil administration, so much that was oppressive and unequal, that he held it to be a duty to speculate on the establishment of justice and freedom, gene-rally, if not with particular applications. The country was threatened by no enemies from without, but they were thought to exist at home; on this or that seat of justice, in the cabinet, in the court; and as Klopstock, by the introduction of the cho-rus of bards into the sacred oaken grove, had given to the German fancy a sort of country and station, as he had beaten the Romans once more by the aid of song, it was natural that, among our youth, bards, called and uncalled, should arise, and, for a time, court the Muse, well or ill, as might happen.

" And we must not be displeased with our poet, whose pure love of country was afterwards so actively, nobly, and variously displayed, if he too occasionally coloured the Rhine with the blood of tyrants, in order to break the slavish bonds of reality.

" But his leaning to French notions of liberty was neither violent nor of long continuance. Soon was our poet repelled by the results of the unfortunate experiment, and he returned, unharmed, to the bosom of moral and civil liberty.

" This disappointment of his hopes frequently gave a colour even to his criticisms on art ; especially, he expressed himself with vehemence, it may be said with harshness, as to those various, irregular, indeterminate attempts, by which German poetry fell, for a while, into confusion. Here he did not appear sufficiently to discriminate, but to visit all with equal condemnation, although, out of this very chaotic struggle, many things worthy of praise arose. Yet it must be acknowledged that such passages and poems are comparatively rare, and, without a key, scarcely intelligible ; for which reason, we must accede to the general justice of our poet's judgements. That so sensitive, retired, and unworldly a nature, should be by no means adequately stimulated, encouraged, and strengthened to cheerful activity, may be readily presumed. But who can say that such a lot has fallen to him ? And thus we find, in many of his earlier poems, touches of a certain dissatisfaction and disquietude, which unconsciously break forth, even through the joyous sound of the catch (*rund-gesang*), and through the cheerful glow of friendship and of love ; and in passages of many an admirable poem, jarringly break the general sympathy. And no less do we observe songs written at a later period, in which gentle murmurs tell of impeded efforts, of stinted growth, of troubled production, of vexations of various kinds ; and portions of life are bewailed as lost. Then, however, he arouses himself, with might and main, fights obstinately, as for his very existence; then he spares no vehemence of language, no weight of invective, when that bright freedom of spirit which he has attained to, that serene glance over the universe, and its moral arrangement which beams forth from the peace within, when the child-like love for Him who guides and governs all, is in any sort darkened, hindered, troubled. If others *will* rob the poet of this feeling of universal, holy complacency; if they *will* set up a peculiar doctrine, an exclusive interpretation, a contracted and contracting principle,—then is his mind moved, even to passion; then does the peaceful man rise up, grasp his weapon, and go forth against errors which he thinks so fearfully pernicious; against credulity and superstition ; against phantoms arising out of the obscure depths of nature, and of the human mind; against reason-obscuring, intellect-contracting dogmas; against decrees and anathemas; against proclaimers of heresy, priests of Baal, hierarchies, clerical hosts, and against their great common progenitor, the Devil himself.

" But ought we to blame such feelings in a man, whose whole mind is penetrated with the conviction, that he, in common with many others, owes the true happiness of his existence to that clear light, which, some centuries ago, diffused itself over the north,—not without the greatest sacrifices on the part of its followers and propagators ?

" Ought we to accede to the apparently fair, but radically false and unfair maxim, which, impudently enough, declares that true toleration must be tolerant, even towards intolerance ? By no means; intolerance is ever active and stirring, and can only be maintained by intolerant deeds and practices.

" Yes; we fully understand the intense vexation and regret of the poet, when, menaced on another side by these gloomy influences, they threaten to rob him of a friend—a friend in the fullest sense of the word. If our poet himself, as we have seen, clings so fondly to objects which cannot even return his affection, how must he attach himself

to the Sympathizing—to men;—to those like himself—to noble and high natures; and count them
among his dearest and richest treasures!

" His mind and his heart early seek enlightened
and light-seeking men. Already do the forms of
Hagedorn and Kleist*, the first removed, and
equally revered fathers of German poetry, hover
in their æsthetic abodes; to them is turned the
glance of their youthful successor; their names
are celebrated in pious hymns. Nor less do we
see the eminent and accomplished living masters
and critics, Klopstock, Lessing, Gleim, Gersten-
berg, Bodmer, Rammler, honoured by their new
competitor, in the lofty consciousness of his own
powers, with manly self-estimation and dignified
modesty. Already we find the names of Stolberg,
Bürger, Boie, Miller, Hölty, bearing friendly testimony to the value of the fame which their country is soon to confer upon them.

" In the midst of this loved and honoured band,
in which time made but few and inconsiderable
chasms, the poet passed his life. He was even so
happy as to interweave the early threads of his
academic youth through the whole texture of his
future life, by friendship, love, relationship, mar-

* Ewald Christian von Kleist, who died in 1759, of
wounds received at the battle of Kunnensdorf.

riage, by unvarying sympathy, by travelling, visits, and letters.

" How, then, must it pain one so amiable, and so favoured by fortune, when not death but failing affection,—when back-sliding into that old soul-enthralling state which our fathers combated with all their might, threatens for ever to sever him from one of his dearest friends! Here his mortification knows no measure; the grief which he feels at so melancholy a breaking-up of his delightful circle is boundless. Nor, indeed, would he know how to rise above this sorrow, did not the Muse here, too, grant him the inestimable power of venting the feelings which oppressed him to the bosom in a sympathizing friend, in a powerful harmonious stream. If we now return from our poet's expression of his general or individual feelings to his descriptive talent, we shall find much to observe.

" A style of poetry devoted peculiarly to na-ture, I may say, to reality, has its rise at that point where the otherwise unpoetical man endeavours to confer a peculiar value on what he possesses,—on what immediately surrounds him. That agreeable form of selfishness when the produce of our own land is the sweetest to us, when we think we can offer our friends no feast so dainty as the fruit which grows in our own garden, is of itself a sort of poetry, which genius and art do but cultivate and polish. They lend to what is the poet's own, not only the peculiar value of partiality, the *pretium affectionis,* but invest it with an universal one, an impressive dignity; and thus does the poet make all that is his the property of his cotemporaries, of the world, and of posterity.

" A deep-feeling, energetic nature produces this talismanic effect by true insight, by affectionate perseverance, by minute detail, by the handling of every circumstance as a Whole in itself; and thus satisfies the indispensable and fundamental necessity for internal keeping; but that is not all; outward means are also required to form a graceful structure out of these materials. These are, language and rhythm. And here it is that our poet gives the highest proofs of his mastery.

" For the zealous study of language, the Low German appears to possess peculiar opportunities. Cut off from every thing ungerman, he hears around him only a soft, agreeable, primitive German; and his neighbours speak kindred languages. And when he approaches the sea, when foreign mariners arrive, the radical syllables of his dialect strike upon his ear, and he receives back from stranger lips much of his own native tongue that had perhaps fallen into disuse with him; and thus accustoms himself to mark the derivation and kindred of words in the intercourses of life, more than can be done by the High German, who borders on nations of a quite different extraction.

" The first part of philology our poet acquires scientifically. The derivation of a word leads him to the consideration of its meaning; and he thus establishes much that is significant, restores misapplied words to their original station, and, if he proceed with quiet caution and accuracy, he is yet not wanting in the courage to employ a hard and generally-avoided expression, in a suitable place.

" From this thorough and perfect estimate of the value of words, from this determinate use of them, arises a compacted and settled language, which, removed from that of ordinary prose, rises imperceptibly into higher regions, and may therefore be esteemed poetic in itself. Here appear the junctions and combinations of words, the position of them to the greatest advantage, which present themselves to the German writer; and we may affirm that invaluable examples are to be found among them.

" And not alone do we admire the bringing to light of these treasures of a tongue, in the deepest sense of the word, noble; but also what the poet, by his high endeavours, and by adherence to the strictest rules, has done for the rhythmus of the language. He was not satisfied with that substantial purity of expression, in which every word is rightly chosen, and not one admits a collateral or ambiguous idea, but denotes its subject, singly and precisely. He requires, for perfection, harmony of sound, graceful and varied structure of the sentence, as it naturally fashions itself in the cultivated mind for the expression of a subject, a sentiment, in a manner perfectly appropriate, and at the same time attractively elegant.

" And here we recognize the eternal service he rendered to German rhythmus, which he raised out of a state of confusion and uncertainty, to the steadiness and determinateness so desirable for the artist. He listened with attentive ear to the high-sounding cadence of Greek antiquity, and, in his hands, the German tongue acquired an equal harmony. In this way did the secret of syllabic measure unfold itself to him; thus did he find the most intimate union between poetry and music; and, under the influence of the friendly society of Schultz, he was enabled theoretically and practically to communicate to his country the fruits of their common efforts.

"Peculiarly agreeable is the study of those poems

which, from their form, present themselves as imitations of the remains of antiquity. It is instructive to observe how the poet proceeds. It is not merely a similar body, laboriously re-constructed; it is rather the same spirit appearing once more to give birth to the same form.

"And as the poet is deeply convinced of the value of a determinate and perfect form, of which he has now obtained complete mastery, he turns these newly recognized demands against his own earlier poems, and corrects and finishes them according to the laws of his late matured perfection.

" Grammarians and technicians are bound especially to acknowledge these his efforts : it only remains for us to add a few touches to the task we undertook ; *i. e.* to discover the poet from his song, the song from the poet.

" Within the compass of these four volumes we find how he gradually formed himself to be so admirable a translator of the works of antiquity.

" By the decisive victory of Form over Matter, which we have praised above, by many poems entirely independent of foreign suggestion, the poet shows us that he has it perfectly in his power to quit the Actual and ascend into the Possible ; to reject the Near and to seize the Distant ; to renounce the Proper and to appropriate the Foreign. And as men were wont to say that, beside the Roman people, a people of statues ennobled the city, so may it equally be said of our poet, that in him a perfectly antique intellectual world is associated to a genuine German practical existence.

" It was his good fortune to devote his youth to the ancient tongues and literature ; to choose them as the business of his life. Not piecemeal, alphabetical knowledge was his aim ; he pressed on, even to actual insight,—to immediate comprehension, of the Past in its truest relations ; he made the Remote present to him, and happily seized the childlike mind with which the earliest civilized nations figured to themselves, with circumscribed fancies, their vast abode the earth, the overarching heaven, the hidden Tartarus ; he saw and felt how it was that they peopled these regions of space with gods, demi-gods, and wondrous forms ; how they assigned to each a place for his dwelling, a path for his wandering. Moreover, attentive to the progress of the human mind, which ceased not to observe, to conclude, to create, the enquirer caused the more perfect conception which we moderns possess of the structure of the universe, and of the earth, as well of its inhabitants, gradually to unfold and mature itself before him. How much fable and history are thereby advanced is no longer hidden from any; and his merit will ever appear the more striking, the more this method obtains on every side, and the more what is collected can be arranged and displayed according to its laws.

" Such are the grounds on which are founded his high claim to attach himself to the eldest of bards, to receive from him poetical consecration, to accompany him in all his wanderings, that he might return back among his countrymen, strengthened and elevated. Thus, without the least renunciation of the Peculiar and Characteristic in himself, did he know how to value what was peculiar and characteristic in every century, in every people, in every poet; and he presented to us the works of antiquity with so practised and masterly a hand, that foreign nations will be constrained henceforward to regard the German tongue with admiration, as a mediator between ancient and modern ages."

Mir trug Lyaeos, mir der begeisternden
Weinrebe Sprössling; als, dem Verstürmten gleich
  Auf ödem Eiland' ich mit Sehnsucht
Wandte den Blick zur Hellenenheimath.

Schamhaft erglühend, nahm ich den heiligen
Rebschoss, und hegt' ihn, nahe dem Nordgestirn,
  Abwehrend Luft und Ungeschlachtheit
Unter dem Glas' in erkargter Sonne.

Vom Trieb der Gottheit, siehe beschleuniget,
Stieg Rankenwaldung, übergewölbt, mich bald
    Mit Blüthe, bald mit grünem Herling,
Bald mit gerötheter Traub' umschwebend.

Im süssen Anhauch träumt' ich, der Zeit entflohn,
Wettkampf mit alterthümlichem Hochgesang.
    Wer lauter ist, der koste freundlich,
Ob die Ambrosiafrucht gereift sey*.

TRANSLATION.

To me brought Lyæos, to me, the inspiriting
shoot of the vine-tree; when like the cast-away
    on desert island, I, with longing,
turned my eyes to my Hellenic home.

Timidly glowing, took I the holy
vine-plant, and fostered it near to the North-star;
    fencing off wind and inclemency,
under the glass, in the husbanded sun.

See, impelled by the Godhead's power, rapidly
shot up the climbing grove, over-arched; me soon
    with blossom, then with green berries,
then with red-blushing bunches, surrounding.

* The reader will understand that these lines are not
Goethe's, but Voss's.

L 2

In the sweet inspiration, dreamed I of times fled;
labour to rival the high song of elder days:
    Let him who pure is, cheerfully taste
if the ambrosial fruit ripened be.

Note 6.

Zigeuner-hauptmann.

      Lumpen und Quark
      Der ganze Mark!
      Sind nicht den Teufel werth!
      Weitmäulichte Laffen
      Feilschen und gaffen,
      Gaffen und kaufen,
      Bestienhaufen!
      Kinder und Fratzen,
      Affen und Katzen!
      Möcht' all das Zeug nicht,
      Wenn ich's geschenkt kriegt'!
      Dürft' ich nur über sie!

Zigeuner-bursch.

      Wetter! wir wollten sie!

Zigeuner-hauptmann.

      Wollten sie zausen!

Zigeuner-bursch.

    Wollten sie lausen !

Zigeuner-hauptmann.

    Mit zwanzig Mann

    Mein wär' der Kram!

I attempted to translate this, but find it impossible to do it in such a way as not greatly to disserve the author.

The *Jahrmarkt zu Plundersweilern* is one of the outpourings of that wild, many-coloured fancy to which Goethe sometimes gave the reins, and which stand in such wonderful contrast with the severe, chaste, antique beauty of his *Iphigenie*, the exquisite tenderness and grace of some of his songs, and the majestic, oracular tone of such poems as *Das Göttliche.* If the portion here extracted be taken to be an expression of Goethe's opinions or feelings towards the mass of mankind, I shall regret having inserted it ; if it be regarded as a proof, among many, that there is no state of mind or feeling which was foreign to Goethe—which he could not understand and give utterance to—I shall rejoice at having given it a place among these few " *pièces justificatives.*"

The persons of the drama are such as a German fair would naturally furnish : a quack doctor and his man, a Tyroler, a Nürnberger, *&c.* with their

wares ; venders of brooms, of cart-grease, of gin-
gerbread ; and an equal variety of buyers. It is
upon this motley group that the sharp -sighted Gipsey,—the outlaw and paria,—wholly devoid of sympathies with any, moralizes thus contemptuously.
Then come a pair of ballad-singers chanting forth
the most edifying common places, beginning,

> " Ihr lieben Christen allgemein
>   Wann wollt ihr euch verbessern ?" &c.

As one might say,

> Good Christians all, both great and small,
> When will you mend your ways ?

which of course draw down the approbation of the
" *Amtmann*," or magistrate.

Other personages and incidents, all described
with wonderful brevity and humour, then glide
over the stage, and we are introduced to " *Hans-
würst*" or Jack-pudding, and his colleague the
" *Marktschreier*," or mountebank, who usher us
into a play on the story of Esther.

Last comes a *Schattenspielmann*, or galantee-
show-man, whose description of the creation and
deluge shows how perfectly familiar Goethe was
with the sort of traditional lore which amused the

simple fathers of the German people. The reader acquainted with the *Wunderhorn* will recognize some features of old friends. The wit in this little drama, or rather succession of scenes, reminds us somewhat of that of Swift; only that it is lighter, more varied, and with a tinge of romance of the simple and poetical character of the middle ages, which it would be absurd to look for in an English writer of the age of Anne. This same wild, fantastic character distinguishes it from the wit of the French school, and allies it with that of Shakespeare.

For the song " *Ich hab' mein Sach,*" it would be far more easy to find parallels in both French and English. · It is indeed a strain of moralizing so old, that a man may run through the whole circle of human disappointments, and say not one new thing.

The gay, vivacious expression of the verse, and the idiomatic language, are gone in the translation, which is consequently a mere lifeless body, and only serves to tell, as children say, " what it is about."

Vanitas ! vanitatum vanitas!

Ich hab' mein Sach auf Nichts gestellt.
Juchhe !
Drum ist's so wohl mir in der Welt.
Juchhe !

Und wer will mein Kamerade seyn,
Der stosse mit an, der stimme mit ein,
   Bei dieser Neige Wein.

Ich stellt' mein Sach auf Geld und Gut.
   Juchhe!
Darüber verlor ich Freud' und Muth.
   O weh!
Die Münze rollte hier und dort,
Und hascht' ich sie an einem Ort,
   Am andern war sie fort.

Auf Weiber stellt' ich nun mein Sach.
   Juchhe!
Daher mir kam viel Ungemach.
   O weh!   .
Die Falsche sucht sich ein ander Theil,
Die Treue macht mir Langeweil:
   Die Beste war nicht feil.

Ich stellt' mein Sach auf Reis' und Fahrt.
   Juchhe!
Und liess mein Vaterlandesart.
   O weh!
Und mir behagt es nirgends recht,
Die Kost war fremd, das Bett war schlecht,
   Niemand verstand mich recht.

Ich stellt' mein Sach auf Ruhm und Ehr.
   Jucbbe!

Und sieh! gleich hatt' ein Andrer mehr.
О weh!
Wie ich mich hatt' hervorgethan,
Da sahen die Leute scheel mich an,
Hatte keinem Recht gethan.

Ich setzt' mein Sach auf Kampf und Krieg.
Juchhe!
Und uns gelang so mancher Sieg.
Juchhe!
Wir zogen in Feindes Land hinein,
Dem Freunde sollt's nicht viel besser seyn,
Und ich verlor ein Bein.

Nun hab' ich mein Sach auf Nichts gestellt.
Juchhe!
Und mein gehört die ganze Welt.
Juchhe!
Zu ende geht nun Sang und Schmaus.
Nur trinkt mir alle Neigen aus;
Die letzte muss heraus!

TRANSLATION.

I have set my mind upon nothing,
Hurrah!
Therefore am I so well in the world,
Hurrah!

And he who will my comrade be,
let him drink with me, let him think with me,
over these lees of wine.

I set my mind upon gold and land,
Hurrah!
On them I lost joy and spirits,
Alas!
The coin rolled hither and thither,
and, if I caught it on the one side,
on the other it was gone.

On women now I set my mind,
Hurrah!
Thence came to me great annoyance,
Alas!
The false one sought another love,
the true one made me very tired,—
the best was not to be got.

I set my mind on journey and travel,
Hurrah!
And left all my fatherland's ways;
Alas!
And nowhere I found true comfort:
the fare was strange, the bed was bad,—
nobody understood me right.

I set my mind on fame and honour,
Hurrah!

And lo, instantly another had more,
    Alas !
When I had made myself famous,
people looked askance at me,—
    I had pleased nobody.

I set my mind on fight and war,
    Hurrah !
And we obtained many a victory,
    Hurrah !
We marched into the enemy's land,
our friends fared not much better,—
    and I lost a leg.

Now have I set my mind on nothing,
    Hurrah !
and the whole world belongs to me,
    Hurrah !
Song and good cheer are coming to an end,
only drink out all the lees,—
    the last must be drained.

NOTE 7.

The scene here alluded to is the one in which the noble, true-hearted Goetz is caught in the toils of his enemies. I insert the translation of Sir Walter Scott, not because I think it gives anything like an adequate idea of Goethe's tragedy, but because it might seem presumptuous to give another. It is moreover interesting to look back upon this early production of the great novelist, and to trace up to this accurate delineation of life in the middle ages, the bent which his genius received.

Goetz is, perhaps, the most attaching of heroes; for the simplicity and kindliness of his heart are equal to its loyalty and bravery, and his unsullied knighthood is utterly without a tinge of *morgue* or of selfishness. We see that the lion-hearted, iron-handed man is as defenceless against the wiles of his enemies, as his own child. Goethe has been reproached, and not always without reason, with the want of dignity and refinement in the characters of his women. Elizabeth and Maria are certainly not, in our sense of the word, "accomplished,"—still less, " fashionable;" but Elizabeth, in her noble simplicity and gentleness, is the fit partner of the noblest of knights, and as brave and high-souled as he; and Maria is worthy to be his sister.

Sir W. Scott's translation is little read; nor indeed is it deserving of more notice than it has received. It is much to be regretted that Goethe's best tragedies are not attempted again. The translation of Tasso I have never seen, but I hear it is feeble. Mr. William Taylor's translation of *Iphigenie* is well known, and is one of the best versions we have of any German poem. Two or three small fragments from this tragedy lately appeared in the New Monthly Magazine. From the signature " F. H." and still more from their beauty, I concluded they were by Mrs. Hemans. They were well calculated to excite a longing desire for more from the same refined and harmonious pen.

GOETZ of BERLICHINGEN.

SCENE—The Council-House at Heilbron.

[*The imperial Commissioners seated in judgement—the Captain and the Magistrates of the city attending.*]

Magistrate.—We have, according to your order, collected the stoutest and most hardy of our burghers to wait in the neighbourhood.

Commissioner.—We will communicate to his Imperial Majesty the zeal with which you have obeyed our illustrious commander.   Are they artizans?

Magistrate.—Smiths, coopers, and carpenters; men with hands hardened by labour—and resolute here— [*Points to his breast.*]

Comm.—'Tis well!

Enter SERJEANT.

Serjeant.—Goetz von Berlichingen waits at the door.

Comm.—Admit him.

Enter GOETZ.

Goetz.—God greet you, my lords!   What would ye with me?

Comm.—First, that you consider where you are, and with whom.

Goetz.—By my faith, I know it well, my lords!

Comm.—You do but your duty in owning it.

Goetz.—From the bottom of my heart!

Comm.—Be seated.   [*Points to a stool.*]

Goetz.—What, there?   Down below?   I can stand; That stool smells of the criminal,—as, indeed, does its whole apparatus.

Comm.—Stand, then.

Goetz.—To business, if you please.

Comm.—We'll go on in order.

Goetz.—I am happy to hear it.—Would every one did as much!

Comm.—You know how you fell into our hands, and are a prisoner at discretion.

Goetz.—What will you give me if I know no such thing?

Comm.—Could I give you good manners, I would do you a good office.

Goetz.—A good office!—can you render any? Good offices are more difficult than the deeds of destruction.

Secretary.—Shall I enter all this on record?

Comm.—Only what is to the point.

Goetz.—Do as you please, for my part.

Comm.—You know how you fell into the power of the Emperor, whose paternal goodness overpowered his justice; and, instead of a dungeon, ordered you to wait your future doom, upon your knightly parole, in his beloved city of Heilbron.

Goetz.—Well—I am here, and wait it.

Comm.—And we are here, to intimate to you his Imperial Majesty's grace and clemency. He is pleased to forgive your rebellion, to release you from the ban, and all well-deserved punishment; provided you do, with suppliant humility, receive his bounty, and subscribe the articles which shall be read unto you.

Goetz.—I am his Majesty's true servant, as ever. One word, ere you go further: My people—where are they?—what is to become of them?

Comm.—That concerns you not.

Goetz.—So may the Emperor turn his face from you in your need! They were my companions, and they are so.—What have you done with them?

Comm.—We owe you no account of that.

Goetz.—Ah! I had forgot :—never was promise kept by you to the oppressed.—But, hush !

Comm.—Our business is to lay the articles before you. Throw yourself at the Emperor's feet, and by humble supplication you may find the true way to save the life and freedom of your associates.

Goetz.—Your paper !

Comm.—Secretary, read it.

Secretary.—[*Reads.*] " I, Goetz of Berlichingen " make public acknowledgement, by these presents, " that I, having lately risen in rebellion against the " Emperor and empire ——"

Goetz.—'Tis false ! I never offended either.

Comm.—Compose yourself, and hear further.

Goetz.—I will not compose myself, and I will hear no further. Let any one arise and bear witness :—Have I ever taken a step against the Emperor, or against the House of Austria ? Have I not, in all my feuds, conducted myself as one who felt what all Germany owes to its head, and what the free knights and feudatories owe to their liege lord, the Emperor ? I should be a liar and a slave, could I be persuaded to subscribe that paper.

Comm.—Yet we have strict orders to persuade you by fair means, or else to throw you into jail.

Goetz.—Into jail ? Me ?

Comm.—Where you may expect your fate from the hands of justice, since you will not take it from those of mercy.

Goetz.—To jail! You abuse the imperial power.—
To jail! That was never his command. What, ye
traitors, to dig a pit for me, and hang out your oath,
your knightly honour, as the lure! To promise me
permission to ward myself on parole, and then to break
your treaty!

Comm.—We owe no faith to robbers.

Goetz.—Wert thou not the representative of my
prince, whom I respect even in the vilest counterfeit,
thou should'st swallow that word, or choke upon it.
I was taken in honourable though private war. Thou
mightest thank God, that gave thee glory, had'st thou
ever done as gallant deeds as the least with which
I am charged. [*The Commissioner makes a sign to the
Magistrates of Heilbron, who go out.*] Because I would
not join the iniquitous confederacy of the great, because
I would not grasp at the souls and livings of the helpless—'tis in this lies my crime! I defended my own
life, and the freedom of my children,—see ye any rebellion in that? The Emperor and empire were blinded to
our hard case, by your flatteries.—I have, God be praised!
one hand, and I have done my best to use it well.

Enter a Party of ARTISANS, armed with halberts and
swords.

Goetz.—What means this?

Comm.—Ye will not hearken. Apprehend him!

Goetz.—Is that the purpose? Let not the man
whose ear does not itch come too near me. One salu-
tation from my trusty iron fist shall cure him of head

ache, tooth ache, and every ache under the wide heaven!
[*They make at him. He strikes one down, and snatches
a sword from another. They stand aloof.*]

Comm.—Surrender!

Goetz. [*With the sword drawn.*]—What! Wot ye not
that it depends but upon myself to make way through
all these hares, and gain the open field? But I will
teach you how a man should keep his word. Promise
to allow me free ward, and I give up my sword, and am
again your prisoner.

Comm.—How! Would you treat with your Emperor sword in hand?

Goetz.—God forbid!—only with you and your worthy
companions! You may go home, good people; here
deliberation is of no avail, and from me there is nothing
to gain, save bruises.

Comm.—Seize him, I say! What! does your allegiance to the Emperor supply you with no courage?

Goetz.—No more than the Emperor supplies them
with plaster, for the wounds which their courage would
earn for them.

A POLICE OFFICER enters hastily.

Officer.—The warder has just discovered, from the
castle tower, a troop of more than 200 horsemen, hastening towards the town. They have already gained
the hill, and seem to threaten an attack.

Comm.—Alas! alas! What can this mean?

A SOLDIER enters.

Soldier.—Francis of Seckingen waits at the drawbridge, and informs you that he has heard how perfidiously you have dealt with his brother-in-law, and how fruitless has been every appeal to the justice of the Council of Heilbron. He is now come to insist upon that justice; and if refused it, he shall fire the four corners of your town within an hour, and abandon it to be plundered by his vassals.

Goetz.—My gallant brother?

Comm.—Withdraw, Goetz! [*He steps aside.*] What is to be done?

Magistrate.—Have compassion upon us and our town! Seckingen is inexorable in his wrath—he will keep his vow.

Comm.—Shall we forget what is due to ourselves and the Emperor?

Captain.—Well said, if we had but men to support our dignity! but as we are, a show of resistance would only make matters worse. We must gain time.

Magistrate.—We had better apply to Goetz, to speak a good word for us. I feel as if the flames were rising already.

Comm.—Let Goetz approach.

Goetz.—What would ye?

Comm.—Thou wilt do well to dissuade thy brother-in-law from his rebellious interference; instead of rescuing thee, he will only plunge thee deeper in destruction, and became the companion of thy fall.

Goetz.—[*Spies Elizabeth at the door, and speaks to her aside.*] Go, tell him instantly to break in, and force his way hither—only, to spare the town. As for the rascals here, if they oppose him, let him use force; there would be no great matter, had he a fair pretext for knocking them all upon the head.

[*Trampling and galloping heard. All the Magistrates show signs of consternation.*]

SCENE changes to the Front of the Council-House, beset by SECKINGEN's Cavaliers. A pause.

Enter SECKINGEN and GOETZ, from the Council House.

Goetz.—This was help from Heaven. How camest thou so much to our wish, and beyond our hope, brother?

Seckingen.—Without witchcraft. I had dispatched two or three messengers to learn how it fared with thee, and heard from them of this villainy. I set out instantly, and now you have the power in your hand.

Goetz.—I ask nothing, but knightly ward upon my parole.

Seckingen.—You are too moderate. Avail yourself of fortune, which for once has placed worth above malice! They were doing injustice; we'll greet them with no kisses for their pains. They have misused the royal authority, and, if I know the Emperor, he will make thee ample reparation. You ask too little.

Goetz.—I have ever been content with little.

Seckingen.—And hence hast thou ever been cut short, even of that little. My proposal is, that they shall release your servants, aud permit you all to return to your castle upon your parole—not to leave it till the Emperor's pleasure be known. You will be safer there than here.

Goetz.—They will say my property is escheated to the Emperor.

Seckingen.—So say we ; but, still, thou mayest dwell there, and keep it for his service till he restores it to thee again. Let them wind like eels in the mud, they shall not escape us ! They will talk of the imperial dignity of their orders. We'll take that risk upon ourselves : I know the Emperor, and have some influence with him ; he has ever wished to have thee in his service ; thou wilt not be long in thy castle, ere thou art summoned to serve him.

Goetz.—God grant it, ere I forget the use of arms !

Seckingen.—Valour can never be forgot, as it can never be learnt. Fear nothing ! When once thou art settled, I will seek the imperial court, where my enterprises begin to ripen. Good fortune seems to smile on them ; I want only to sound the Emperor's mind. The towns of Triers and Pfalz as soon expect that the sky should fall, as that I should come down upon their heads ; but I will come, like a storm of hail on the unsuspecting traveller ; and if I am successful, thou shalt soon be brother to a prince. I had hoped for thy hand in this undertaking.

Goetz. [*Looks at his hand.*]—O ! that explains to me the dream I had the morning that I promised Maria to Weislingen. I thought he professed eternal fidelity, and held my iron hand so fast that it loosened

from the arm.   Alas ! I am at this moment more helpless and defenceless than when it was shot from me.
Weislingen !   Weislingen !

Seckingen.—Forget the traitor ! We will darken his
prospects and cross his plans, till shame and remorse
shall gnaw him to death.   I see, I see the downfall of
my enemies—of thine, Goetz :—only half a year !

Goetz.—Thy soul soars high ! I know not how, but
for some time, no fair prospects have smiled upon mine.
I have been in distress—I have been a prisoner ere now,
but never before did I experience such a depression.

Seckingen.—Fortune gives spirits.   Come, let us to
the periwigs; they have had our conditions long enough,
we must call for their resolution.   [*Exeunt.*

NOTE 8.

Heinrich Meyer was a native of Zürich.   He
enjoyed, for many years, the closest intimacy with
Goethe, who, as appears in the text, had a singular esteem for him.   They were at Rome together, and travelled home together, in 1797, when
they made the tour of the small Swiss cantons.
Mention of him occurs in the *Italiänische Reise,*

in the *Zweyter Aufenthalt in Rom,* and in the *Tag-und-Jahres Hefte.* Goethe's first interview with him was in the chapel of the Quirinal, on All Soul's day, 1786; " for," observes Goethe, " the feast of All Souls is the feast of all artists, in Rome."

" The artist who gave me the information I sought," says he " was Heinrich Meyer, a Swiss, who has been studying here for some years, draws admirably in sepia, from the antique, and is well skilled in the history of art."

In the *Tag-und-Jahres Hefte* (A. D. 1794) I find the following :

" As inmate of my house, I now once more possessed my oldest Roman friend, Heinrich Meyer. The recollection and prosecution of our Italian studies furnished us with daily occupation and amusement. During our last residence at Venice, we had come to a thorough understanding of each other anew, and our union was the more intimate and perfect."

1795.—" Meyer went back to Italy ; for, though war had already broken out with violence in Lombardy, the other parts were as yet untouched, and we lived in the visionary hope of being able to renew the years 87 and 88. His departure robbed me of all conversation on the arts of design ; and even the preparations I made to follow him led me into other pursuits."

1797.—"Friend Meyer constantly sent me most interesting letters from Italy. My preparations for following him compelled me to pursue various studies, the documents (*Acten Stücke*) regarding which are still of great service. While working out the history of Florentine art, Cellini became an important personage to me; and to make my-myself a thorough Florentine citizen, I took the resolution of translating his autobiography—especially, because it seemed that it might be of use to Schiller for his *Horen.*"

1798.—" From this, however," (some poetical work) " I was diverted to the arts of design, which Meyer's return from Italy just then rendered peculiarly interesting. I continued the life of Cellini, as a resting point in the history of the 18th century."

1802.—" My domestic circumstances at Weimar underwent an important change. Friend Meyer, who, ever since 1792, with the exception of some few years, had shared my roof and table, and had enlivened and benefitted me by his instructive society and invaluable counsels, quitted my house in consequence of a matrimonial connection. Nevertheless, the necessity for unbroken sympathy and concert overcame the short distance which divided us : a mutually co-operative influence in each other's pursuits remained in full activity, and experienced neither hindrance nor pause."

1803.—" As I have, all my life long, been so much on my guard against nothing as against empty words; and as a phrase which did not express some real thought or feeling appeared to me intolerable in others, impossible to myself, I suffered positive pain in translating Cellini, for which the immediate sight of objects described, or alluded to, was indispensable. I heartily regretted that I had not better employed my first journey through Florence, or my second visit to it, in taking a more perfect and accurate view of modern art. Friend Meyer, who had acquired the most fundamental knowledge of this subject, in 1796-7 helped me to the utmost of his power. Yet I still longed after the opportunity, no longer granted me, of seeing with my own eyes.

" I fell upon the thought, that if Cellini's own medals, on which he piques himself so much, were not to be found, some cotemporary ones might, perhaps, be obtained.

" Luckily I heard of an auction at Nürnberg, at which coins of the fifteenth, sixteenth, seventeenth,

and eighteenth century were to be sold, and I succeeded in getting possession of the whole mass.
It contained not only the original series of Popes
from Martin V. to Clement XI., consequently to
the first quarter of the eighteenth century, but
also cardinals, priests, philosophers, learned men,
artists, celebrated women, — all in sharp, unin-
jured specimens,—some stamped, some cast; but,
strange and lamentable to say, among so many
hundreds, not one Cellini.

" This stimulated me to get all the historical
knowledge I could; I searched Bonanni, Mazuchelli
and others, and thus laid the foundation for a quite
new branch of learning."

Since I collected the fragments above, I have
been informed by a friend, a native of Zürich, that
Meyer was entirely self-educated, and had no
advantages in early life but those which nature
gave him.

NOTE 9.

As a further illustration of Goethe's manner of viewing the traditional and formular instruction given at schools and colleges, I subjoin nearly the whole scene from which the lines in the text are extracted. Readers of German will be aware that in the later editions the words "*Spottet ihrer selbst*" are substituted for "*Bohrt sich selber Esel.*"

I have taken this scene from an unpublished version of Faust (by the translator of Von Savigny's "Vocation of our Age for Legislation and Jurisprudence)." He has not aimed at making a rhythmical translation, which, from the nature of the restraints it imposes, must of necessity be often rather a paraphrase than a translation, but has endeavoured to give the exact and literal meaning of the original; a meaning often lost sight of by others, and never without enormous loss.

In the following scene, the young student comes, full of ardour, to put himself under the tuition of Faust, whom Mephistophiles has just succeeded in utterly disgusting with the business of a teacher. He refuses to see the boy, on which Mephistophiles assumes his form and character, and this dialogue takes place.

A STUDENT enters.

Student.—I am but just arrived, and come, full of devotion, to address and become acquainted with a man whom all name with reverence.

Mephistophiles.—I am flattered by your attention. You see a man like many others. Have you made any enquiry elsewhere?

Student.—Interest yourself for me, I pray you. I come with every good disposition, a little money, and youthful spirits; my mother could hardly be brought to part with me, but I would fain learn something worth learning in the world.

Mephist.—You are here at the very place for it.

Student.—Honestly speaking, I should be glad to be out again. These walls, these halls, are by no means to my taste. The space is exceedingly confined; there is not a tree, nothing green to be seen; and in the halls, on the benches,—hearing, sight, and thinking fail me.

Mephist.—It all depends on habit. Thus at first the child does not take kindly to the mother's breast, but soon finds a pleasure in nourishing itself. Just so will you daily experience a greater pleasure at the breasts of Wisdom.

Student.—I shall hang delightedly upon her neck: do but tell me how I am to attain to it.

Mephist.—Tell me, before you go further, what faculty you fix upon?

Student.—I would wish to be profoundly learned,

and should like to comprehend what is upon earth or in heaven,—science and nature.

Mephist.—You are here upon the right scent; but you must not suffer your attention to be distracted.

Student.—I am heart and soul in the cause. A little relaxation and pastime, to be sure, would not come amiss on bright summer holidays.

Mephist.—Make the most of time, it glides away so fast. But method teaches you to gain time. For this reason, my good friend, I advise you to begin with a course of logic. In this study the mind is well broken in,—laced up in Spanish boots,—so that it creeps circumspectly along the path of thought, and runs no risk of flickering, ignis-fatuus like, in all directions but the right. Then many a day will be spent in teaching you that one, two, three, is necessary for that which formerly you hit off at a blow, as easily as eating and drinking. It is with the fabric of thought as with a weaver's master-piece, where one treadle moves a thousand threads, the shuttles shoot backwards and forwards, the threads flow unseen; ties, by thousands, are struck off at a blow. Your philosopher,—he steps in and proves to you, it must have been so : the first would be so, the second so, and therefore the third and fourth so; and if the first and second were not, the third and fourth would never be. The students of all countries put a high value on this, but none have turned weavers. He who wishes to know and describe any thing living, seeks first to drive the spirit out of it; he has then the parts in his hand: only, unluckily, the spiritual bond is wanting. Chemistry terms it *encheiresis naturæ,* and mocks herself without knowing it.

Student.—I cannot quite comprehend you.

Mephist.—You will soon improve in that respect, if you learn to reduce and classify all things properly.

Student.—I am so confounded by all this; I feel as if a millwheel was turning round in my head.

Mephist.—In the next place, before any thing else, you must set to at metaphysics. There, see that you conceive profoundly what is not made for human brains. A fine word will stand you in stead for what enters and what does not enter there. And be sure, for the first half year, to adopt the strictest regularity. You will have five lectures every day. Be in as the clock strikes. Be well prepared beforehand with the paragraphs carefully conned, that you may see the better that he says nothing but what is in the book; yet write away as zealously as if the Holy Ghost were dictating to you.

Student.—You need not tell me that a second time. I can imagine how useful it is. For what one has in black and white, one can carry home in comfort.

Mephist.—But choose a faculty.

Student.—I cannot reconcile myself to jurisprudence.

Mephist.—I cannot much blame you. I know the nature of this science. Laws descend, like an inveterate hereditary disease; they trail from generation to generation, and glide imperceptibly from place to place. Reason becomes nonsense: beneficence, a plague. Woe to thee that thou art a grandson! Of the Law that is born with us—of that, unfortunately, there is never a question.

Student.—You increase my repugnance. Oh, happy he whom you instruct! I should like to study theology.

Mephist.—I do not wish to mislead you. As for this science, it is so difficult to avoid the wrong way; there is so much hidden poison in it, which is hardly to be distinguished from the medicine. Here, again, it is best to attend but one master, and swear by his words. Generally speaking, stick to words; you will then pass by the safe gate into the temple of certainty.

Student.—But there must be some meaning connected with the word.

Mephist.—Right! Only we must not be too anxious about that: for it is precisely where meaning fails that a word comes in most opportunely. Disputes may be admirably carried on with words; a system may be built with words; words form a capital subject for belief; a word admits not of an iota being taken from it.

Student.—Your pardon,—I detain you by my many questions, but I must still trouble you; Would you be so kind as to add an instructive word or two on medicine? Three years is a short time, and the field, God knows, is far too wide. If one has but a hint, one can feel one's way along further.

Mephist. [*Aside.*]—I begin to be tired of the prosing style. I must play the devil properly again. [*Aloud.*]

The spirit of medicine is easy to be caught; you

study through the great and little world, to let things go on in the end—as it pleases God. It is in vain that you wander about scientifically, no man learns more than he can ; he who avails himself of the passing moment—that is the proper man. You are tolerably well built, nor will you be wanting in boldness, and if you do but confide in yourself, other souls will confide in you. * * * * * * * * * * * * *

Student.—There is some sense in that ; one sees at any rate the where and the how.

Mephist.—Gray, my dear friend, is all theory, and green the golden tree of life.

Student.—I vow to you, all is a dream to me. Might I trouble you another time to hear your wisdom speak upon the grounds ?

Mephist.—I am at your service, to the extent of my poor abilities.

Student.—I cannot possibly go away without placing my common-place book in your hands. Do not grudge me this token of your favour !

Mephist.—With all my heart. [*He writes and gives it back.*]

Student.—[*Reads.*] " Eritis sicut Deus, scientes bonum et malum." [*He closes the book reverentially, and takes his leave.*]

Mephist.—Only follow the old saying and my cousin the snake, and some time or other you, with your likeness to God, will be sorry enough.

Note 10.

I do not find this name in Goethe's works, and conclude that it is misspelt. In the *Tag-und-Jahres Hefte*, 1808, I find this:

"The presence of Kaaz, the admirable landscape-painter of Dresden, brought me great delight and instruction, especially from the ease and mastership in which he transformed my dilettanteish sketches into very fair pictures. By the manner in which he combined the beauty of water and body colours, he brought me out of my fantastic whims to a purer style. And as proofs how the society of a master raises and bears us into another element, I preserve some leaves of that time, which mark to me, like points of light, that under such circumstances we are capable of things which both before and after seem to us impossible."

1811.—"The drawings of Kaaz, who had been too early removed from the world, were laid before me. Princess Caroline of Mecklenburg, who was distinguished for her taste and execution in landscape-painting, became possessor of a part of them."

NOTE. (omitted) Page 77.

I find this passage about dogs in the *Tag-und-Jahres Hefte*. The latter part is amusing to those who have had the luck to be waked in the night by the "*ungeheure Ton*," as Goethe most justly calls it, of the nocturnal horn he mentions. I once heard it in a most obscure little town in Franconia, just on the borders of the Black Forest, in which every thing was of a piece—antique, primitive, and catholic. The sound of the horn under my window, startling me out of the sleep that follows on a whole day's travelling, I shall not soon forget. After his blast, the watchman recited four lines—a sort of invocation or blessing, which was clearly a remnant of the middle ages. I jumped up and opened my window to hear it, and only regret I did not write it down.

What follows happened to Goethe in Göttingen. After bitter complaints of the zeal and assiduity of the young lady of the house in which he lodged, in practising music, especially at night, he adds—

" Other noises, of a different kind, gave cause for desperation : a number of dogs collected around the corner house, and their incessant barking was insupportable. To drive them away, I seized upon the first missile that came to hand, and in this way many a *Cornu Ammonis* of the Heinberg, carefully collected by my son, flew out of the window at these unwelcome rest-breakers :—and generally in vain. For when we thought we had scared them all away the barking continued just as before. At last we discovered that a great dog, belonging to the house in which we lodged, placed himself upright at a window over our heads, and thence held up a conversation with his friends.

" But this was not all; I was waked out of a deep sleep by the monstrous tone of a horn, which sounded exactly as if it was blowing between the curtains of my bed. A watchman had his station under my window, where he diligently discharged this part of his functions. And thus I was doubly and trebly unhappy; for all his colleagues, at all the corners of the streets which led to ours, answered him, proving to us by the most frightful and alarming noises that they were keeping watchful guard over the tranquillity of our slumbers.

"Now awaked my morbid irritability of nerves— and nothing was left for it but to enter into a negotiation with the police, which had the extraordinary courtesy and kindness to put to silence first one, and then several other, of these horns, at the desire of the odd stranger, who was very near playing the part of the uncle in Humphrey Clinker, whose impatient irritability was goaded to madness by the sound of hunting horns."

This little corroborative poem is from the *Elegien*.

Manche Töne sind mir Verdruss, doch bleibet am
    meisten
Hundegebell mir verhasst; kläffend zerreisst es mein
    Ohr.
Einen Hund nur hör' ich sehr oft mit frohem Behagen
Bellend kläffen, den Hund, den sich der Nachbar erzog.
Denn er bellte mir einst mein Mädchen an, da sie sich
    heimlich
Zu mir stahl, und verrieth unser Geheimniss beinah'.
Jetzo, hör' ich ihn bellen, so denk ich nur immer: sie
    kommt wohl!
Oder ich denke der Zeit, da die Erwartete kam.

TRANSLATION.

Many sounds are an annoyance to me, but above all is the barking of dogs hateful—yelping it splits my ear. One dog alone do I hear very often with joyful delight, yelp barking; the dog which my neighbour has reared. For once he barked at my maiden when she privily stole to me, and almost he betrayed our secret. Now, when I hear him bark, I think always—then she is coming! or I think of the time when the expected one came.

Here, too, is one of his Epigrams:

Wundern kann es mich nicht das Menschen die Hunde
    so lieben;
Denn ein erbärmlicher Schuft ist, wie der Mensch, so
    der Hund.

TRANSLATION.

It cannot surprise me that men love dogs so much;
For dog, like man, is a pitiful sneaking rogue.

NOTE. (omitted) Page 84, line 4.

I cannot find this expression in Diderot, nor can any one tell me where it is to be met with. I am the more sorry for this, because it would be important to see the very word Diderot uses— whether or not it be " *existera*."

For neither we nor the French have any word

corresponding to that which Goethe uses—viz. *werden*,—which signifies not only a future existence, but a progress in or towards it. The Latin *fiet* would exactly answer to the German. A friend has pointed out to me the following curious coincidence.

Southey, in his *Omniana*, (p. 262,) mentions "a *philosopher*" who held this opinion. " He was perfectly satisfied that there is no God at present, but he believed there would be one by and by : for, as the organization of the universe perfected itself, a universal mind, he argued, would be the result. This he called the system of progressive nature. He explained it to me with great zeal, when we were walking over the very ground where, thirteen years afterwards, the battle of Coruña was fought. Light lie the earth upon him ! He was a kind-hearted man, and all his wishes were for the welfare and improvement of mankind ; but it had been well for him if his other intellectual vagaries had produced as little mischief as his system of progressive nature."

NOTE 11.

PROMETHEUS.

I annex the whole of this celebrated poem, and such a translation of it as I could accomplish. I have held to the measure of the lines as nearly as possible, and, with very few exceptions, each line contains neither more nor less than the corresponding one of the original.

The magnificent roll of some lines, the passionate abruptness, and the melancholy tenderness of others, are unfortunately lost to the English reader. Goethe's mastery over language—over the expressions suited to every conceivable subject of thought or feeling, is among his wondrous endowments. The loftiest and the meanest; the most stately severity and the wildest extravagance; words that create a shudder by their unearthly dissonances, and others that fall like soft dew upon the heart, or that bring to our senses the fresh, reviving brightness of a spring morning—each and all are "familiar in his mouth as household words,"—nor is it possible to say in which he excelled, so perfect is each in its kind. The poems which may be classed with the *Prometheus* are, the

Ganymede, the *Gränze der Menschheit* (Limits of Humanity), and, finer than all, *Das Göttliche* (the Godlike),—all in irregular, unrimed metre. Rime, indeed, would have been wholly out of keeping with the perfectly Greek tone of these poems.

In the *Dichtung und Wahrheit* (book 15) we find the following account of the state of mind and train of thought which gave birth to this extraordinary production. Two passages, which I have marked in italics, struck me as affording glimpses of Goethe's inmost peculiarity of mental structure.

" The common burthen of humanity, which we have all to bear, more or less, must lie heaviest on those whose mental powers are the earliest and the most widely unfolded. We may grow up under the sheltering care of parents and of kindred, we may lean on brethren and on friends, we may be amused by acquaintances, we may be made happy by those we love ;—yet, ' to this conclusion do we come at last,'—that man is turned back upon himself; and it appears as if even the Divinity had chosen to place himself in such a relation to man, that He cannot always respond to his reverence, confidence, and love,—at least, not in the moments of the greatest urgency.

" Often enough in my youth I had experienced that, in the moments of our uttermost need, a voice cried aloud to us, ' Physician, cure thyself!' and how often was I not forced, in bitterness of heart to sigh, ' I must tread the wine-press alone.'

" When I looked around for some support to my self-dependence, I found that the securest foundation for it was my productive talent. For some years, this never deserted me for an instant. What met my waking senses, frequently recurred to me by night, in regular, connected dreams; and as soon as I opened my eyes, either a wondrous new Whole, or a part of what had already appeared, presented itself to them.

" I commonly wrote every thing at break of day; but in the evening too, nay, deep into the night, when wine and social intercourse raise the animal spirits, people might require of me what they would. I wanted nothing but an occasion that had some character in it, and I was prepared and ready.

" And now, when I thought over this gift of nature, and found that it belonged to me as a quite peculiar possession, and could neither be helped nor hindered by any foreign influence, I willingly sought to make it the ground or basis of my whole existence. *This notion transformed itself into an image;* the old mythological figure of Prometheus occurred to me, who, severed from the Gods, peopled a world from his workshop. I felt most distinctly that nothing considerable could be produced without self-isolation. Those things of mine which had gained such applause were children of loneliness; and since I had stood in wider connection with the world there had been no want of vigour and brilliancy of invention; but the execution halted, because, neither in prose nor in verse, had I what could properly be called a style; and in every fresh work, according to what the subject might be, I was always forced to make tentatives and experiments beforehand.

"And since I had here to decline, nay to exclude, all help from man, I also severed myself, Promethean-wise, even from the Gods; and *so much the more naturally, since, with my character and manner of thinking, one subject of contemplation invariably swallowed up or drove away all others.*

"The fable of Prometheus had a living existence in me. I cut down the old Titanic garment to my own stature, and, without further reflection, began to write a poem in which is depicted the incongruous relation in which Prometheus stood to the new Gods; inasmuch as he had formed men with his own hand, had animated them with the aid of Minerva, and had founded a third dynasty. And truly, the Gods then in power had abundant cause to complain, since they might thus be regarded as beings unjustly interposed between Titans and men.

"In this strange composition appears, as Monologue, that poem which is become important in German poetry as having furnished the occasion which led Lessing to declare his opposition to Jacobi on some weighty points of thought and feeling. But though (as it thus appeared) this poem may be made the subject of moral and religious discussion, yet does it properly belong to the province of poetry alone. The Titans are the extravagance of Polytheism, just as the Devil may be regarded as the extravagance of Monotheism; but the latter is no figure for poetry, any more than the One God to whom he is placed in opposition. Milton's Satan, though finely drawn, has always the disadvantage of a subaltern position; inasmuch as his whole efforts are directed towards the destruction of the magnificent creation of a higher Being. Prometheus, on the contrary, stands on a vantage ground, from having the power to create and to model, in defiance of higher beings. It is a beautiful thought, too, and most consonant with poetry, to trace the creation of man, not to the highest rulers of the world, but to an intermediate being, who, however, as descendant of the elder dynasty, is majestic and important enough for such a work. And, indeed, the Greek mythology affords exhaustless riches of divine and human symbols.

" The titanic, gigantic, heaven--storming character, however, afforded no material for my vein of poetry. Rather did it suit me to depict that peaceful, plastic, and ever-patient resistance, which owns a superior power, but seeks to equal it. Yet even the more daring of the race were my saints. Received into the society of the Gods, they would not behave obsequiously enough,—incurred the anger of their hosts and patrons, as insolent guests, and drew upon themselves a miserable sentence of condemnation. I pitied them. The ancients had already regarded their destiny and condition as profoundly tragical : I placed them in the back ground in my *Iphigenie* as members of a colossal opposition, and I am indebted to them for a part of the effect which that piece had the good fortune to produce."

PROMETHEUS.

Bedecke deinen Himmel, Zeus,
Mit Wolkendunst,
Und übe, dem Knaben gleich,
Der Disteln köpft,
An Eichen dich und Bergeshöhn;

Musst mir meine Erde
Doch lassen stehn,
Und meine Hütte, die du nicht gebaut,
Und meinen Herd,
Um dessen Gluth
Du mich beneidest.

Ich kenne nichts aermeres
Unter der Sonn', als euch, Götter!
Ihr nähret kümmerlich
Von Opfersteuern
Und Gebetshauch
Eure Majestät,
Und darbtet, wären
Nicht Kinder und Bettler
Hoffnungsvolle Thoren.

Da ich ein Kind war,
Nicht wusste wo aus noch ein,
Kehrt' ich mein verirrtes Auge
Zur Sonne, als wenn drüber wär'
Ein Ohr, zu hören meine Klage,
Ein Herz, wie mein's,
Sich des Bedrängten zu erbarmen.

Wer half mir
Wider der Titanen Uebermuth?
Wer rettete vom Tode mich,
Von Sklaverey?
Hast du nicht Alles selbst vollendet,
Heilig glühend Herz?
Und glühtest jung und gut,

Betrogen, Rettungsdank
Dem Schlafenden da droben?
  Ich dich ehren? Wofür?
Hast du die Schmerzen gelindert
Jc des Beladenen?
Hast du die Thränen gestillet
Je des Geängsteten?
Hat nicht mich zum Manne geschmiedet
Die allmächtige Zeit
Und das ewige Schicksal,
Meine Herrn und deine?
  Wähntest du etwa,
Ich sollte das Leben hassen,
In Wüsten fliehen,
Weil nicht alle
Blüthenträume reiften?
  Hier sitz 'ich, forme Menschen
Nach meinem Bilde;
Ein Geschlecht, das mir gleich sey,
Zu leiden, zu weinen,
Zu geniessen und zu freuen sich,
Und dein nicht zu achten
Wie ich!

TRANSLATION.

Curtain thy heavens, Zeus,
With clouds and mist;
And exercise thine arm,

(Like a boy cropping thistles),
On oaks and mountain-tops.
Yet must thou leave
My earth still standing;
And my hut, which thou buildedst not,
And my hearth,
Whose flame
Thou enviest me.

   I know nought more pitiful
Under the sun, than you, ye gods!
You nourish scantily
With forced offerings,
And breath of prayer,
Your majesty;
And would starve, were not
Children and beggars
Hope-deluded fools.

   When I was a child,
Unknowing where to turn,
I raised my wilder'd eye
To the sun, as if there, above, were
An ear to hear my plaint;
A heart, like mine,
To pity the oppressed.

   Who succoured me
Against the Titans' insolence?
Who rescued me
From death, from slavery?
Didst thou not, thou thyself, achieve it all,

Holily-glowing heart?
And didst thou not, in young and credulous love,
Deceived one, pour out thy warm thanks for safety
To the sleeper there, above?

    I reverence thee!—Wherefore?
Hast *thou* ever lightened the woes
Of the heavily laden?
Hast *thou* ever stilled the tears
Of the troubled in spirit?
Did not almighty Time,
And eternal Fate
(My Lords and thine),
Fashion me Man?

    Dreamedst thou, belike,
I should hate life,—
Flee to the desert,
Because not all
Dream-blossoms ripened?

    Here I sit—form Men
After my image:
A race that may be like me—
That may suffer,—weep,—
Enjoy,—rejoice,—
And heed not thee—
Like me!*

---

  * This last line is bad, and I know not how to better
it. The German is, *As I.* I should have preferred that,
if I had not feared it would have been too repulsive to
an English ear.—*Transl.*

Note 12.

This is the answer of Faust, to Margaret's anxious and affectionate enquiries into the state of his religious opinions and belief.

Wer darf Ihn nennen?
Und wer bekennen:
Ich glaub' Ihn.
Wer empfinden
Und sich unterwinden
Zu sagen: ich glaub' Ihn nicht?
Der Allumfasser,
Der Allerhalter,
Fasst und erhält er nicht
Dich, mich, sich selbst?
Wölbt sich der Himmel nicht da droben?
Liegt die Erde nicht hierunten fest?
Und steigen freundlich blickend
Ewige Sterne nicht hier auf?
Schau' ich nicht Aug' in Auge dir,
Und drängt nicht alles
Nach Haupt und Herzen dir,
Und webt in ewigem Geheimniss
Unsichtbar sichtbar neben dir?
Erfüll' davon dein Herz, so gross es ist,
Und wenn du ganz in dem Gefühle selig bist,
Neun'es dann wie du willst,

Nenn's Glück! Herz! Liebe! Gott!
Ich habe keinen Namen
Dafür! Gefühl ist alles;
Name ist Schall und Rauch,
Umnebelnd Himmelsgluth.

Who can name Him?
And who declare
I believe in Him?
Who can feel,
And dare affirm
I believe in Him not?
The All-encompassing,
The All-sustaining,
Encompasses, sustains he not
Thee, me, Himself?
Spreads not the heav'n its vault above?
Lies not the earth stedfast beneath?
And climb not the eternal stars
Beaming with friendly light?
Doth not mine eye gaze in the depths of thine?
Doth not all that is
Press on thy head and heart,
And visibly, invisibly,
Weave its mysterious web eternally around thee?
Fill with it now thy heart—howe'er capacious—

And when that feeling mounts to perfect bliss,
Then call it as thou wilt—
Call it joy! heart! love! God!
I have no name for it—
Feeling is all—
Name is but sound and vapour,
Inshrouding heaven's glow!

As there exist translations of this sublime and celebrated passage, it seems necessary that I should explain the presumption of giving one of my own; and this I can only do by annexing those which are before the public, and pointing out the reasons which led me to regard them as wholly unsatisfactory.

Lord Leveson Gower's is as follows:

Who could himself compel
To say he disbelieves
The Being whose presence all must feel so well?
The All-creator,
The All-sustainer,
Does he not uphold
Thyself, and me, and all?
Does not yon vaulted Heaven expand
Round the fast earth on which we stand?
Do we not hail it, though from far
The light of each eternal star?
Are not my eyes in yours reflected?

And, all these living proofs collected,
Do they not flash upon the brain,
Do they not press upon the heart,
The trace of Nature's mystic reign?
Inhale the feeling till it fill
The breast, then call it what you will.
Call it an influence from above,
Faith, heaven, or happiness, or love,—
I have no name by which to call
The secret power,—'tis feeling all.

It begins with one of the most singular examples of the misapprehension, not only of the particular passage in question, but of the *whole* genius of an author, that I remember to have seen. Goethe says:

" Who may name Him?
And who affirm
I believe in Him?
Who can feel,
And dare declare
I believe in Him not?"

Now the translator has taken not the slightest notice of the first three lines, and has thus completely succeeded in destroying not only all that is remarkable in the sentiment, but all that is characteristic of Faust or of Goethe. For the multi-

tude have, in all ages, been ready enough to ask
" who can feel, and dare declare, I believe on Him
not ?" But what the poet puts into the mouth of
Faust—the insatiable craver after *knowledge,*—
is, the expression of the eternal problem, the in-
superable difficulty, the unappeasable doubt, which
render it impossible to men like him to affirm
either belief or unbelief on such a subject. If Lord
Leveson Gower had any scruples about exhibiting
this state of the mind of a man who had been made
desperate from unsatisfied desire of knowledge,
"Faust" was surely an extraordinary choice. That
he was not sensible of his omission, and did not
see that, by taking away half, he destroyed the
whole, is hardly credible.

All-creator is not only no translation of *Allumfasser,* but stands in direct and most important
contradiction to it, and is utterly at variance with
the pantheistical tendency and character of the
whole passage.

" The Being whose presence all must feel so well,"
there is no authority for in the original.

> " Does he not uphold
> Thyself, and me, *and all ?*"—

is as prosaic and vulgar as it is unfaithful; Goethe
says, " Thee, me, *Himself.*"

The lines—

> " And all these living proofs collected,"

and the three succeeding, are surely very wide of the original.

No allusion is made to the *unsichtbar sichtbar neben dir*:

> " The trace of Nature's mystic reign "

is not like any thing in the original.

> " Inhale the feeling till it fill
> The breast, then call it what you will,"

is feeble and vulgar.

> " Call it an influence from above,
> Faith, heaven, or happiness or love,—"

Here again the translator has most unfortunately disguised the original. Of " influence from above " Goethe says not a word,

> " Call it as thou wilt————
> Call it happiness, heart, love, *God*—"

the concluding word being the very one to which all Gretchen's enquiries tended, and that which contains the sum of what Faust designs as his answer. If the translator found any thing irreverent in this line, I cannot but think he quite misunderstood Goethe. At all events, it seems to me contrary to the morality which ought to regulate our dealings with foreign authors, to garble and distort their meaning, particularly on points so delicate. If the public cannot be made to under-stand what the duties of translators are, it is at least always possible to append a note disclaiming participation in this or that opinion. The degree to which the last line loses in poetry, I need not point out. I regret the deficiences of this passage the more, because there is much to admire in Lord Leveson Gower's translation. The ease and grace of the versification are often remarkable, and some passages are very happily rendered.

Madame de Staël, in her *Allemagne*, has given a version of this passage, which, being in prose, has not the excuse afforded by the restraints of verse. Yet hers is quite as offensively inaccurate ; and if the one is deadened by English one-sided-ness, the other is made ridiculous by French affec-tation and *phrases*.

" Qui peut nommer la *divinité*, et dire, je la con-*çois ?* Qui *peut être sensible et ne* pas *y croire ?* Le *soutien de* cet univers, n'embrasse-t-il pas toi, moi, *la nature entière ?* Le ciel ne s'abaisse-t-il pas en pavillon sur nos têtes ? La terre n'est elle pas inébranlable sous nos pieds ? et les étoiles eter-nelles, du haut de leur sphère, ne nous regardent-elles pas *avec amour ?* Tes yeux ne se réflechissent-ils pas dans mes yeux *attendris?* Un mystère éternel, invisible et visible, n'attire-t-il pas *mon cœur vers le tien?* Remplis ton âme de ce mystère, et, quand tu éprouves la felicité suprème *du sentiment,* appelle-la cette felicité, cœur, amour, Dieu,— n'importe. Le sentiment est tout; les noms ne sont qu'un vain bruit, une vaine furnée qui obscurcit la clarté des cieux."

Where did Madame de Staël find *"la Divinité?"* Goethe expressly says he has "no name" for that of which he speaks. *"Je la conçois"* has no resemblance to the meaning. *"Qui peut être sensible,"* is a poor dilution of the original, and gives it a sentimental, mawkish air, wholly inappropriate. *"Le soutien de cet univers"* is all foisted in,— and, like *"la divinité,"* above, destroys the sublime mystery and simplicity which are conveyed by the *Ihn* and *Er* of the original. *"La nature entière"* is like Lord L. Gower's "and all,"—an unpardonable substitution for *"sich selbst."* *"Mes yeux attendris"*—another *phrase* out of a French novel:— Faust does not talk so. The next sentence has not the least resemblance to the original; Goethe says, *"drängt nicht alles nach Haupt und Herzen dir?"* This mysterious pressure of the Great Whole on the head and heart is converted into, *"n'attire-t-il pas mon cœur vers le tien."* This it is, to fall into the hands of the French. Faust, like the heroes of antiquity, must speak according to the prescribed *formulæ* of love-making. The Faust of Goethe says nothing about " *mon cœur.*"

" *De ce mystère*" is an interpolation:—"*la felicité suprème du sentiment*" sounds to me very unlike the original, but I suppose it is the nearest French for it.

"*Appelle-la cette felicité,*" is not accurate.

The conclusion, which Lord L. Gower has so unaccountably spoiled, is faithfully rendered, except that " *gluth,*" glow, or fire, is not " *clarté.*"

I am afraid these observations on two persons of high reputation may be thought to come with a very ill grace from so obscure a pen. If there is any appearance of conceit or presumption in them, I shall extremely regret it; but it seemed to me greater presumption to prefer a translation of my own without assigning some reason. The assertion that these translations were bad, appeared equally to require proof, and I could not say what I thought of them, and say less. The morality of translating has, unfortunately, been understood and practised by no people ·but the Germans, and it is time that the conscientious endeavour to understand and render an author should not be all on one side.

N 5

Note 13.

I think the reader will thank me for subjoining
this elegant poem.

Lili's Park.

Ist doch keine Menagerie
So bunt, als meiner Lili ihre!
Sie hat darin die wunderbarsten Thiere,
Und kriegt sie 'rein, weiss selbst nicht wie.
O wie sie hüpfen, laufen, trappeln,
Mit abgestumpften Flügeln zappeln,
Die armen Prinzen allzumal,
In nie gelöschter Liebesqual!

Wie heiss die Fee?—Lili?—Fragt nicht nach ihr!
Kennt ihr sie nicht, so danket Gott dafür.

Welch ein Geräusch, welch ein Gegacker,
Wenn sie sich in die Thüre stellt
Und in der Hand das Futterkörbchen hält!
Welch ein Gequick, welch ein Gequacker!
Alle Bäume, alle Büsche scheinen lebendig zu werden:
So stürzen sich ganze Herden
Zu ihren Füssen; sogar im Bassin die Fische
Patschen ungeduldig mit den Köpfen heraus:
Und sie streut dann das Futter aus

Mit einem Blick—Götter zu entzücken,
Geschweige die Bestien. Da gehts an ein Picken,
An ein Schlürfen, an ein Hacken;
Sie stürzen einander über die Nacken,
Schieben sich, drängen sich, reissen sich,
Jagen sich, ängsten sich, beissen sich,
Und das all um ein Stückchen Brod,
Das, trocken, aus den schönen Händen schmeckt,
Als hätt' es in Ambrosia gesteckt.
Aber der Blick auch! Der Ton!
Wenn sie ruft: Pipi! Pipi!
Zöge den Adler Jupiters vom Thron;
Der Venus Taubenpaar,
Ja der eitle Pfau sogar,
Ich schwöre, sie kämen,
Wenn sie den Ton von weitem nur vernähmen.

Denn so hat sie aus des Waldes Nacht
Einen Bären, ungeleckt und ungezogen,
Unter ihren Beschluss herein betrogen,
Unter die zahme Compagnie gebracht,
Und mit den andern zahm gemacht:
Bis auf einen gewissen Punkt, versteht sich!
Wie schön und ach! wie gut
Schien sie zu seyn! Ich hätte mein Blut
Gegeben, um ihre Blumen zu begiessen.

"Ihr sagtet *ich!* Wie? Wer?"
Gut denn, ihr Herrn, g'rad'aus: Ich bin der Bär;

In einem Filetschurz gefangen,
An einem Seidenfaden ihr zu Füssen,
Doch wie das alles zugegangen,
Erzähl' ich euch zur andern Zeit;
Dazu bin ich zu wüthig heut.

Denn ha! steh' ich so an der Ecke,
Und hör' von weitem das Geschnatter,
Seh' das Geflitter, das Geflatter,
Kehr' ich mich um
Und brumm',
Und renne rückwärts eine Strecke,
Und seh' mich um
Und brumm',
Und laufe wieder eine Strecke,
Und kehr' doch endlich wieder um.

Dann fängts auf einmal an zu rasen,
Ein mächt' ger Geist schnaubt aus der Nasen,
Es wildzt die innere Natur.
Was, du ein Thor, ein Häschen nur!
So ein Pipi! Eichhörnchen, Nuss zu knacken,
Ich sträube meinen horst'gen Nacken,
Zu dienen ungewöhnt.
Ein jedes aufgestutzte Bäumchen höhnt
Mich an! ich flieh' vom Boulingreen,
Vom niedlich glatt gemähten Grase;
Der Buchsbaum zieht mir eine Nase,
Ich flieh' ins dunkelste Gebüsch hin,

Durch's Gehäge zu dringen,
Ueber die Planken zu springen!
Mir versagt Klettern und Sprung,
 Ein Zauber bleit mich nieder;
Ein Zauber häkelt mich wieder,
Ich arbeite mich ab, und bin ich matt genung,
Dann lieg' ich an gekünstelten Cascaden,
Und kau' und wein' und wälze halb mich todt,
Und ach! es hören meine Noth
Nur porzellanene Oreaden.

Auf Einmahl!   Ach, es dringt
Ein seliges Gefühl durch alle meine Glieder!
Sie ist's, die dort in ihrer Laube singt!
Ich höre die liebe, liebe Stimme wieder,
Die ganze Luft ist warm, ist blüthevoll.
Ach! singt sie wohl, dass ich sie hören soll?
Ich dringe zu, tret' alle Sträuche nieder,
Die Büsche, die Bäume weichen mir,
Und so—zu ihren Füssen liegt das Thier.
Sie sieht es an: " Ein Ungeheuer! doch drollig!
Für einen Bären zu mild,
Für einen Pudel zu wild,
So zottig, täpfig, knollig!"
Sie streicht ihm mit dem Füsschen über'n Rücken;
Er denkt im Paradiese zu seyn.
Wie ihn alle sieben Sinne jücken!
Und Sie sieht ganz gelassen drein.
Ich küss' ihre Schuhe, kau' an den Sohlen,

So sittig, als ein Bär nur mag;
Ganz sachte heb' ich mich, und schwinge mich ver-
    stohlen
Leis' an ihr Knie—Am günst'gen Tag
Lässt sie's geschehn, und kraut mir um die Ohren,
Und patscht mich mit muthwillig derbem Schlag;
Ich knurr', in Wonne neu geboren;
Dann fordert sie mit süssem, eitlem Spotte:
Allons, tout doux! eh la ménotte!
Et faites serviteur,
Comme un joli seigneur!
So treibt sie's fort mit Spiel und Lachen;
Es hofft der oft betrogne Thor;
Doch will er sich ein Bisschen unnütz machen,
Hält sie ihn kurz, als wie zuvor.

Doch hat sie auch ein Fläschchen Balsamfeuers,
Dem keiner Erde Honig gleicht,
Wovon sie wohl einmal, von Lieb' und Treu' erweicht,
Um die verlechzten Lippen ihres Ungeheuers
Ein Tröpfchen mit der Fingerspitze streicht,
Und wieder flieht, und mich mir überlässt,
Und ich dann, losgebunden, fest
Gebannt bin, immer nach ihr ziehe,
Sie suche, schaudre, wieder fliehe—
So lässt sie den zerstörten Armen gehn,
Ist seiner Lust, ist seinen Schmerzen still;
Ha! manchmal lässt sie mir die Thür halb offen stehn,
Seitblickt mich spottend an, ob ich nicht fliehen will.

Und ich!—Götter, ist's in euren Händen,
Dieses dumpfe Zauberwerk zu enden;
Wie dank' ich, wenn ihr mir die Freiheit schafft!
Doch sendet ihr mir keine Hülfe nieder—
Nicht ganz umsonst reck' ich so meine Glieder:
Ich fühl's! Ich schwör's! noch hab' ich Kraft.

TRANSLATION.

There is really no menagerie
so gay as my Lili's.
She has in it the strangest beasts,
and gets them in she knows not how herself.
Oh, how they jump, and run, and tramp!
How they flap with their clipped wings!—
The poor dear Princes, all *péle-méle*,
in a never-extinguished love-torment!

What is the fairy called?—Lili?—Ask not after her!
If you know her not, thank God therefore.

What a bustle, what a cackle,
when she comes to the door,
·and holds the food-basket in her hand!
What a squeaking, what a quacking!
Every tree, every bush, seems to be alive.
Thus do whole troops rush
to her feet.   Even the fish in the ponds

splash impatiently, with their heads out of the water.
And then she strews the food about,
with a look—to ravish gods,—
much more beasts.   Then begins a picking,
a gobbling, a pecking.
They tumble over each others necks;
shove each other, squeeze each other, pull each other,
drive each other, frighten each other, bite each other,
and that,—all for a little bit of bread,—
which, dry as it is, out of her beautiful hands,
tastes as if it had been steeped in ambrosia.
But the look, too!—the tone!—
when she calls " Pipi, Pipi!"—
would draw the eagle from Jupiter's throne;
the pair of doves from Venus;
nay, even the vain peacock;—
I would swear they would come,
If they heard *that* tone, from ever so far.

For thus has she enticed hither, out of the night of
        woods,
a bear, unlicked and untutored,
under her rule;
brought him into the tame company,
and made him tame like the others—
to a certain pitch—(understood of course).
How beautiful,—and ah! how kind —
seemed she to be!   I would have given my blood,
only to water her flowers!

"I?" say you, "How? Who?"
Well then, good sirs, to be plain, I am the bear,—
caught in a net,—
bound with a silken cord, at her feet.
But, how all that came to pass,
I will tell you another time :—
for that I am too furious today.

For ah! I stand thus in a corner,
and hear from afar the noise ;
see the fluttering and flapping ;
turn myself round
and growl,
and run backwards a bit,
and look round me,
and growl,
and run again a bit,
and at last,—I return.

Then, all at once, rage stirs within me ;
a fierce spirit snorts from out my nose !
my inmost nature storms.
" What! thou be a fool,—a coward hare ?
Such a " Pipi !"—a little squirrel to crack nuts !"
I shake my brushy neck,
to serve, unused.
Every little upstart tree mocks at me :
I flee from the bowling-green ;
from the pretty smooth-shaven grass :

The box-tree turns up its nose at me.
I flee away to the darkest thicket,
break through the hedge,
leap over the pales;—
a spell lies like lead upon me;
forbids me to scramble or to leap:
a spell draws me back again;—
I wear myself out, and when I am tired enough
I lie down by the artificial cascade,
and champ, and weep, and toss myself half dead;
and ah! my anguish is heard
by porcelain Oreads alone.

All at once,—ah, what a blissful feeling
rushes through every limb!
'Tis she who sings there, in her bower!
I hear the dear, dear voice again:
The whole air is warm—is redolent of bloom.
Ah! does she then indeed sing that I may hear her?
I rush forward—trample down all the bushes,—
the shrubs, the trees, bend before me,
and thus—at her feet lies the beast.
She looks at him—"A monster, but yet droll!
For a bear too mild,
For a poodle too wild;
so shaggy, clumsy, cumbersome!"
She strokes his back with her little foot;—
he thinks himself in paradise.
How all his seven senses reel!

and *she*—looks down quite carelessly.
I kiss her shoe ; I gnaw the sole
as gently as ever a bear can.
Softly I raise myself up, and by stealth I throw myself
lightly on her knee. On a favourable day
she suffers it, and scratches me under the ear,
and pats me with wantonly heavy slap ;—
I growl, new-born in extacy.
Then cries she, in sweet triumphant sport,
Allons, tout doux ! eh la ménotte !
et faites serviteur,
comme un joli seigneur !
Thus goes she on with jest and laugh.
The oft-deluded fool hopes on ;
but should he grow importunate,
she holds him in, tight as before.

But she has, too, a little flask of balsam-fire—
which no honey on earth equals,—
with which she sometimes, softened by his love and
        truth,
on the parching lips of her monster
puts a little drop with the tip of her finger,
and then runs away, and leaves me to myself.
and I then, though loosed, am spell-bound :
I follow ever after her,
seek her, shudder, flee again :—
Thus does she let the poor disturbed one go ;
is heedless of his pleasures—of his pains :—

Nay, many a time she leaves the door half open,
and looks archly askance at me, as if to ask if I will.not
    escape.

And I!—Ye gods! it is in your hands
to end this tantalizing witchery!—
How should I thank you, if you would give me freedom!
Yet send me down no help :—
Not quite in vain do I thus stretch my limbs;
I feel it! I swear it! I have yet strength.

Note 14.

Amalie, daughter of Duke Charles of Brunswick
Wolfenbüttel, born October, 1739. During the latter half of the last century, this remarkable woman
was the presiding spirit of a court which, as a nur-
sery of art, may be compared to that graced by the
presence of Ariosto and Tasso. She it was who
afforded to men of letters that encouragement and
support they looked for in vain from the mightier
princes of the empire; to her they were indebted
for a point of union, and for an adequate provision.
Nor was it only as a munificent patroness, or as

an enlightened and accomplished judge of literature and art, that Amalie has a claim to universal gratitude.

Married in her seventeenth year, to Duke Ernst August Constantine, she was left a widow in her nineteenth. By a wise administration, she found means to remedy the calamitous consequences of the seven years' war; to accumulate in her treasury a considerable sum of money without imposing any additional burthens on her subjects, and to avert from them the consequences of the famine which desolated Saxony in 1773.

Scarcely, however, had she provided for these most urgent necessities of her people, than she turned her attention to the circumstances which alone ennoble existence. She founded new institutions for their intellectual improvement, and perfected those already in existence. She appointed the illustrious Wieland governor to her son (the late duke), and attracted men of the highest talent to Weimar—Herder, Göethe, Seckendorf, Knebel, Böttiger, Bode, Musæus, and, more lately, Schiller.

It could be only by the union of the rarest qualities of heart and mind, that the princess of so small a state could succeed in assembling around her more distinguished men than were to be found in any cotemporary court, whatever were its powei or splendour. That her personal character contributed more to this than her rank or station, is proved by the circumstance that she continued to be surrounded by the same persons after she had resigned the government into the hands of her son, in 1775. Her palace at Weimar, her country houses at Tieffurth and Ettersburg, never ceased to be the *rendezvous* of literary men and travellers of merit.

A tour in Italy, which she made in 1798, in company with Goethe, heightened her taste for the arts. Thus did this true heiress of the noble qualities and the love of science, which distinguished the house of Brunswick, win the glory of having afforded honour and encouragement to the most illustrious writers of Germany.

The 14th of October, 1806, broke her heart. She survived it but a few months.

Abridged from the Conversations-Lexicon.

———

In the *Tag-und-Jahres Hefte,* (A.D. 1807,) I find the following notice.

" Shortly after this, the Duchess Amalie quitted her native land—which, to her, was shaken to its foundations,—nay, ruined. To all, this was cause of mourning; to me, of peculiar grief. A hasty little memoir, put together rather officially than in any higher and more deep-felt sense, is a mere acknowledgment for how much more I shall remain indebted to her memory."

This slight sketch will be found annexed. It cannot, indeed, be regarded as any adequate expression of Goethe's sentiments.

" To the Memory of the most illustrious lady and princess, ANNA AMALIE, dowager Duchess of SACHSEN -WEIMAR and EISENACH, born Duchess of BRAUNSCHWEIG and LUNEBURG. 1807.

" If the life of the great of this world, so long as it pleases Heaven to prolong it, ought to serve as an example to the rest of mankind, (whereby constancy in misfortune, and beneficent activity in prosperity, may be more widely diffused abroad,) the consideration of a remarkable career must needs be of great importance; since a brief survey of the virtues and the deeds of the departed may be presented to the emulation of every one, as a most precious gift and most noble object of emulation.

" The life of the princess whose memory we are met to commemorate deserves to be engraven on the remembrance of all, but especially on that of such as had formerly the happiness of living under her government, and, more recently, under that influence which she never ceased to exert, as Mother of her country (*Landesmutter*);—on whom she conferred so many benefits, and whom she honoured with her favour and her friendship.

" Sprung from a house, rich from its remotest ancestry, in the Renowned, the High-minded, and the Valiant; niece of a king, the greatest man of his time; surrounded, from childhood, by relations in whom greatness of mind was hereditary,— who scarcely knew any other object of desire or spring of action than such as were honourable, and deserving of the admiration of posterity; in the midst of a court full of mental activity, and continually advancing in civilization, and of a city distinguished for its various institutions for the cultivation of art and science, she was early conscious of the germs of an answering superiority in herself, and delighted in the education which she received from the most excellent instructors, who subsequently gave lustre to the church and to letters.

" She was early removed from the place of her

birth by her matrimonial connection with a young prince, with whom she began life under the brightest auspices. A son was the fruit of this union (1757), and was the centre of a thousand joys and hopes; but his father's pleasure in him was destined to be short. The duke died before his child was two years old. A second son did not see the light till after his death.

" Guardian of two infants,—herself not yet of age,—she found herself, at the breaking out of the seven years' war, in a most anxious situation; bound, as princess of the empire, to adhere to the side which had declared itself against her illustrious uncle, and herself pressed upon by the proximity of military operations. She was, however, somewhat tranquillized by a visit from the great general and monarch. Her states experienced considerable annoyance, but no destructive ravages. At length arrived the wished-for peace; and her first cares were those of a two-fold mother,—for her country, and for her sons. With unwearied patience and gentleness she laboured to implant all that was good and useful, even where it would not immediately take root. She supported and fed her people during a protracted and frightful famine. Every act and decree of her reign was distinguished by a just, free, and noble spirit.

" In the interior of domestic life, her tenderest cares were devoted to her sons. Instructors of the highest worth and merit were placed about them, and she thus drew around her an assemblage of the most eminent men, and laid the foundations of all that was destined to have so important and beneficial an influence, not only on her own peculiar country, but on the whole German Fatherland.

" Whatever can give grace or charm to life, she sought, with wise moderation, to collect around her; and she thought with joy and confidence of delivering up the government she had administered so conscientiously, into the hands of her illustrious son (1774), when the unlooked-for disaster of the burning of the palace of Weimar changed the anticipated pleasure into mourning and distress. But here also she displayed her native character; and after making every arrangement that could alleviate, nay improve, the consequences of this calamity, she surrendered the government into the hands of her eldest son, now of age, and retired, full of honour and dignity, to the enjoyment of a less anxious existence.

" Her regency was the source of manifold benefits to the country; she had converted even misfortunes into occasions of improvement. She encouraged and employed all who displayed capacity for public usefulness. Jurisprudence, political economy, policy*, acquired certainty, consistency, development. An entirely new spirit had come over court and city. Eminent foreigners, learned men, artists, resorted to it as visitors or as residents. The free use of a large library was granted to the public; a good theatre was supported; and the rising generation excited to culture of the mind and taste. The state of the university of Jena was enquired into. The liberality of the princess rendered practicable all the projects submitted to her; and thus was this institution placed on a secure basis, and rendered susceptible of yet further improvements.

" With what joyful feelings must she now see all her earlier wishes fulfilled above her hopes and expectations, under the government of her indefatigable son, while his happy marriage gave the promise of a posterity worthy of her !

" The tranquil consciousness of having done her duty,—of having fulfilled her task,—accompanied her into the repose of private life, in which she was happy, surrounded by art and science, and by the natural beauties of her residence. She delighted

---

* Policy—*i. e.* all that relates to police in the more extensive meaning of the term.—*Transl.*

in the conversation of persons of talent; and sought occasions of forming connexions of this kind, of maintaining them, and of turning them to account: indeed there is no one of any note connected with Weimar whose powers were not, sooner or later, called forth in her circle. Thus did she prepare herself for a journey across the Alps, where she sought health and a milder climate; for she had, shortly before, had an attack which threatened her life. She anticipated the highest enjoyment from the actual perception of that perfection of art, of which she had long had a divining sense,—especially in music, which she had studied scientifically in early life; and from a new extension of her views of life by the acquaintance and society of the distinguished and accomplished persons, native and foreign, who graced those fortunate regions, and who exalted every hour of social intercourse into a remarkable epoch in existence.

" Many enjoyments awaited her when she returned, adorned and enriched with the treasures of art and of experience. We hoped that, as a compensation for so many sufferings and privations, her life would now glide on in a calm and lengthened old age.

" But it seemed otherwise to the All-directing. She had deeply felt the various trials which had attended her course through life;—the early loss of two heroic brothers, killed in battle*; of a third who died devoting himself for others; of a beloved absent son; and, more recently, of a brother who was her guest, and of a great grandson of extraordinary hope and promise. Yet had her courage and strength of mind never forsaken her; she had always commanded herself and resumed the thread of life.

" But in these latter times, when pitiless war, after so long sparing us, at length fell upon us and upon her; when, to snatch her beloved grandchildren from the midst of the wild tumult, she fled from her dwelling and encountered the dangers and difficulties of travel; when she beheld the calamities which had befallen the exalted house with which she was connected by blood, and those which menaced her own, and learned the death of her last remaining loved and honoured brother; when she saw all the hopes, all the expectations of her youth, which had rested on the securest claims, on the well-

---

* In the ducal vault of Brunswick nine of the coffins are marked by the badge which tells that they fell in battle. That of the prince mentioned above, who lost his life in the attempt to save some persons perishing in an inundation, has received the same distinction.— *Transl.*

earned glory of her family, dashed to the ground on every side; then, it seemed, her heart could resist no longer, and her courageous spirit lost its counterpoise to the pressure of earthly powers. Yet did she remain like herself—externally calm, pleasing, graceful, compassionate and sympathizing; and no one of those around her could anticipate that the hour of her release was so near. She made no complaints of illness—she seemed hardly to suffer—she departed out of the company of her people as she had lived. (1807.)

" Her death ought to afflict us only as the Necessary, the Inevitable; not to be embittered by accidental, distressing, gloomy accessories. And to which of us, at the present moment, when the remembrance of past, united to the fear of future, evil, troubles and appals many a spirit, is not such a picture of firm, serene resignation consolatory and supporting? Which of us can say, my sorrows were equal to hers? And if there be any one who can institute so sad a comparison, he, too, must feel strengthened and encouraged by so lofty an example.

" Yes, we return to our first observation :—

" This is the prerogative of the noblest natures—that their departure to higher regions exercises a no less blessed influence than did their abode on earth; that they lighten us from above, like stars by which to steer our course—so often interrupted by storms; that those to whom we turned in life as the Beneficent, the Helpful, now attract our longing, aspiring glance as the Perfected, the Blessed."—(*From Vol. xxxii. of Goethe's works, last edition.*)

NOTE 15.

See Madame de Staël's *Allemagne*. The suppressed scene described by Falk was afterwards published, as most readers of German are aware, in the second part of Faust. It was however considerably altered.

NOTE 16.

Friedrich von Schlegel, younger brother of the accomplished and celebrated translator of Shakspeare and Calderon, was born at Hannover in 1772. Though destined to commerce, he received a liberal education, and, in his sixteenth year, prevailed on his father to allow him to devote himself to literature. He studied at Göttingen and Leipsig. His first important work was the *Griechen und Römer*, to which is annexed an essay on the Platonic Diotima, and on the representations of female character in the Greek poets. In this work he gave evidence of that extensive erudition, that originality of thought, and that power over historico-critical weapons, which he afterwards displayed in the field of ancient and modern poetry.

In 1799 he published his *Lucinde*, a work of fancy, sentiment, and reflection. Rarely have opinions been more divided than on its merits. The author himself, by leaving it unfinished, seems to have admitted the justice of the sentence which condemned it, as a dangerous attempt to give an air of refinement to sensuality.

In 1800 he began to lecture on philosophy at

Jena, and was greatly admired. In 1802, he gave lectures on philosophy in Paris, and devoted himself with great assiduity to the study of the southern and oriental tongues. In 1808 he published his work, *Über die Sprache und Weisheit der Indier* (on the language and wisdom of the Indians). He also studied the old French romances, and published a collection of romantic poems of the middle ages. Having returned to Germany, he proceeded to Vienna, where he became Imperial Secretary at the Archduke Charles's head quarters, and contributed greatly by his proclamations to rouse the spirit of the country. Shortly after, he became a Roman catholic. In 1820 he undertook a periodical work, called *Concordia*, with a view of reconciling the different opinions on church and state, but it did not succeed. In 1827 he gave lectures on the philosophy of life : part of them are printed, and contain a sort of popular philosophy for the higher classes. The literary revolution which was brought about by the intellectual Dioscuri, though it has left traces enough, has been rendered more obnoxious to censure by the folly of the so-called *Schlegelianer*, or Schlegelites, than by the founder of the sect himself, to whom it is impossible to deny great depth and extent of knowledge, and a polished form of statement.—(*Abridged from the Conversations-Lex-icon.*)

Since I extracted the above from the *Conversa-tions-Lexicon*, I have been favoured with the following remarks on the character and works of Friedrich von Schlegel, by Mr. Adolf Heller, a gentleman attached to the Prussian Embassy here, to whom I am glad to avow my obligations for much valuable assistance.

" Friedrich von Schlegel is one of the most distinguished of those men whose whole life is an inward conflict. His thirst after truth led him to the study of philosophy; and while his brother August Wilhelm devoted himself exclusively to the cultivation of the *form* of poetry, Friedrich occupied himself with the *matter*. His first considerable work was the much censured *Lucinde*, a fantastic and dreamy attempt to exalt and sublimate sensual love. Traces of the study of Greek art and literature, received in a mind full of youthful enthusiasm, are frequent and obvious throughout this early production. His imagination was exalted and refined by the Greek poets and by Plato's dialogues, but this feeling was adulterated and defaced by so much of the impurity of modern times that the author failed to gain the sympathy and approbation of the public. The book was generally looked upon as dangerous.

"F. Schlegel next appeared to greater advantage in a periodical book, called the *Athenæum*, to which he, his brother, and Novalis, were the chief contributors. The origin of that æsthetico-critical school of which they may be regarded as the founders, dates from this period. Their philosophical leader was Fichte, whose *Wissenschaftslehre* (system of Philosophy) Friedrich Schlegel regarded as the *non plus ultra* of human enquiry. He called that, and the French revolution, "the two great tendencies of the age." All that was not in conformity with the maxims of this school was rejected with philosophical disdain. Even Schiller's merits were denied by its disciples. But it was against Kotzebue and Iffland, whose plays then enjoyed the most extensive popularity, that they took the field with the greatest ardour. Kotzebue sought to revenge himself in some coarse and absurd farces, in which he endeavoured to render the overstrained enthusiasm of the æsthetic school ludicrous. The Æsthetickers, however, gained a complete victory over Kotzebue, though not by their own might. They were politic enough to ally themselves with Goethe, to express the highest admiration for him, and thus to secure a portion of the universal consideration he enjoyed. It was at this time that Goethe and Schiller published the famous *Xenien* which gave the death blow to their shallow and superficial adversaries. The Schlege-lites now entrenched themselves behind the former of these two illustrious poets, though they renewed their attacks upon Schiller; but this noble-minded man troubled himself not about such criticisms, and held on his simple, serene course. To him, and to the brilliant success which crowned his labours, we chiefly owe it that the critical tyranny of their school was not completely established in Germany.

" Tieck, a friend of Schlegel, was unquestionably a great and formidable member of the confederation. He endeavoured to dethrone Schiller, because he regarded Shakspeare as the sole true model in dramatic art. It is much to be regretted that a man endowed with such a high, and rich, and graceful genius should have plunged so deeply into polemical discussion.

" The æsthetico-critical school now sought and found a new point of union. The Schlegels, Tieck, and Novalis wrote in a strain of profound admiration of the forms of catholicism. They lauded mystical philosophy, represented the middle ages and the institutions of chivalry as the highest and most glorious form of human society, and wrote sonnets to the Virgin Mary. Friedrich Schlegel was at this time occupied with the poetical romances and troubadour songs of Provence and the south of Europe. Tieck followed his example. Though it is matter of congratulation that they did not obtain a victory over their opponents, it must be admitted that they are entitled to our gratitude for the treasures of romantic poetry which they brought into notice; and thus perhaps formed the genius of an Uhland.

" Meanwhile the mischief they did was great. They appear to have combined in the attempt to render catholicism once more the reigning church; and however romantic this may sound, it is certain that Friedrich Schlegel (who was then in the Austrian service) and Tieck, adopted the catholic faith. Novalis did not renounce Protestantism, but his tendency to mysticism in religion was favourable to the cause of his friends.

" The sound mind of the German nation repugned these pernicious vagaries; though traces of them are to be discerned in the latest philosophical writings. The pantheistical tendency of Schelling's philosophy was not opposed to this school; even Schiller unconsciously fell under the suspicion of having evinced a leaning to catholicism in his

Marie Stuart. Goethe, between the years 1820 and 1830, declared himself frankly and decidedly for Protestantism, and nothing remained to the Schlegels, after this abortive attempt at changing the opinions of the nation, but to betake themselves to some other field of action.

" A. W. von Schlegel devoted himself to the study of the Sanscrit language and poetry, and oriental literature generally. Friedrich wrote his " Lectures on the History of Philosophy," and shortly before his death, his *Concordia,* wherein he proceeds upon the idea of the unity of church and state.

" He was a ' conservative;' nay, more,—he would have retrograded. His predilection for the forms of the middle ages appears through everything he did.

" Nevertheless, there is great talent in his *Concordia,* and the opposite errors and delusions of the French revolution, and of ultra liberalism, conduce very powerfully to give an advantageous colour to his side of the question.

" But the flame of his genius had now blazed up for the last time, and had brightened only to be extinguished for ever. With his physical life, his literary existence had also reached its term. He will not live, because he was not independent,—

self-sustained. He never succeeded in creating any thing original and complete. But he certainly contributed greatly to give a direction to the spirit of his age; and it is worthy of notice, that he had more in him than he gave out. The agitated and stormy period in which he lived found him too weak in *character* to maintain an erect and stedfast posture. We are of opinion, however, that he was sincerely persuaded of the rectitude of his endeavours, though perhaps his persuasion was aided by a little personal vanity, and a little ambition. The Austrian court had ennobled him, and it appears to us in every point of view lamentable that a man of his genius should have permitted himself to be regarded as a political agent."—(*Ad. H.*)

Note 17.

I am obliged to a friend for calling my attention to the singular coincidence between the passage in the text and the following stanzas from *Don Juan*. The conversation reported by Falk passed in 1808. *Don Juan* was published in 1819. I insert it as matter of curiosity, though I entirely object to the tone of the whole passage, and to the unworthy and unappretiating mention of such names as Wordsworth, Southey, and Coleridge.

Canto XI.

XLV.

In twice five years " the greatest living poet,"
  Like to the champion in the fisty ring,
Is called on to support his claim, or shew it,
  Although 'tis an imaginary thing.
Even I—albeit I'm sure I did not know it,
  Nor sought of foolscap subjects to be king,—
Was reckoned, a considerable time,
The grand Napoleon of the realms of rhyme.

XLVI.

But Juan was my Moscow, and Faliero
  My Leipsic, and my Mont Saint Jean seems Cain :
" La belle Alliance" of dunces down at zero,
  Now that the Lion's fall'n may rise again :
But I will fall at least as fell my hero ;
  Nor reign at all, or as a monarch reign ;
Or to some lonely isle of Jailors go,
With turncoat Southey for my turnkey Lowe.

XLVII.

Sir Walter reigned before me; Moore and Campbell
　Before and after; but now grown more holy,
The Muses upon Sion's hill must ramble
　With poets almost clergymen, or wholly;
　　＊　＊　＊　＊　＊　＊　＊　＊　＊　＊　＊

XLVIII.

　　＊　＊　＊　＊　＊　＊　＊　＊　＊　＊　＊

XLIX.

Then there's my gentle Euphues, who, they say,
　Sets up for being a sort of moral me;
He'll find it rather difficult some day
　To turn out both, or either, it may be.
Some persons think that Coleridge hath the sway,
　And Wordsworth has supporters, two or three;
And that deep-mouthed Bœotian " Savage Landor "
Has taken for a swan rogue Southey's gander.

L.

John Keats, who was killed off by one critique,
　Just as he really promised something great,
If not intelligible,—without Greek,
　Contrived to talk about the Gods of late,
Much as they might have been supposed to speak.
　Poor fellow! His was an untoward fate:
'Tis strange the mind, that very fiery particle,
Should let itself be snuffed out by an article.

LI.

The list grows long of live and dead pretenders
  To that which none will gain—or none will know
The conqueror at least; who, ere Time renders
  His last award, will have the long grass grow
Above his burnt-out brain, and sapless cinders.
  If I might augur, I should rate but low
Their chances :—*they're too numerous, like the thirty* **
Mock tyrants, when Rome's annals waxed but dirty.

LII.

This is the literary lower Empire,
  Where the Prætorian *bands take up the matter ;—*
A " dreadful trade," like his who " gathers samphire,"
  The insolent soldiery to soothe and flatter,
With the same feelings as you'd coax a vampire.
  Now, were I once at home, and in good satire,
I'd try conclusions with those Janizaries,
And show them what an intellectual war is.

Don Juan, Canto XI.

* This allusion and that in the next stanza are the
most singular coincidences.

NOTE 18.

Novalis, whose real name was Friedrich von Hardenberg, was born on the paternal estate in the Graffschaft of Mansfeld, in 1772, and died at Weissenfels, in 1801.

From his earliest years, a love of the Good and the Beautiful were instilled into him by his excellent parents. He studied philosophy at Jena, and law, at Leipsig and Wittenberg. After visiting the school of Mines at Freiberg, he was appointed director of the salt-works in the electorate of Saxony. At this period he became the friend and intellectual ally of Tieck and the Schlegels. Just as he was about to be appointed to a considerable post in Thuringia, he expired in his father's house, in the arms of his friend, Friedrich Schlegel.

Unquestionably he was a poet, in the holiest sense of the word. His knowledge was various; in law, in natural science, in the higher mathematics, and in philosophy; but poetry predominated over every thing. Soul and Fancy were mirrored in all his works, consisting, unfortunately, chiefly of fragments—mere indications of what he aimed at. All are penetrated with the holy beauty of the Christian faith, with the mild and tolerant spirit of which he was imbued. His deep thoughts were clothed in the utmost simplicity of form. It is a great loss to our literature that his *Heinrich von Ofterdingen,* the originality and beauty of which has been pointed out by his friend Tieck, remained unfinished. Hardenberg intended, after the completion of this novel, to write six others, in which he meant to give all his views on physics, on civil life and action, on history, politics, and love. The *Lehrlinge zu Lais* is the commencement of this great series. But his genius and character were most nobly displayed in the ' Hymns to Night,' with the execution of which, too, he was best satisfied. The greater half of the second part of his works (Berlin, 1814, two vols.), consists of fragments, in which his profound and many-sided mind speaks with the most touching tenderness. He had conceived the project of an encyclopediacal work, in which Experience and Ideas should mutually illustrate, support, and animate each other, in the various sciences. — (*Abridged from the Conversations-Lexicon.*)

No translation of any part of Novalis's works has come in my way; nor is he mentioned in Mr. William Taylor's Survey of German Poetry. A few fragments, with which I had been peculiarly struck, appeared, among others, in the New

Monthly Magazine, more than two years ago. However imperfectly translated, enough of them remains to prove their great beauty, and, I fear, their distastefulness to the generality of English readers.

Many of my readers are probably acquainted with the beautiful article on Novalis which appeared in the Foreign Review, from the pen of Mr. Carlyle, to whom all lovers of German literature are so deeply indebted. The peculiar character of Mr. Carlyle's genius, tastes, and sentiments fit him to be the expositor of such men as Novalis and Jean Paul. What is darkness to the crowd would be made clear to him by the light of his own pure, noble, and unworldly spirit.

I must confess, however, that on a superficial reading of Novalis, he appeared to me to *affect* darkness. It is easy to see how unpalateable his tendency towards the Unreal must be to Goethe.

I have given no note on Tieck, because any adequate account of his genius and works would occupy too much space; and because I think he is better, though very imperfectly, known to England. As a writer of *Märchen*—Fairy Tales—he is unapproachable. His descriptions have a freshness like that of Chaucer, and his fancy is as wild and boundless as it is graceful. His devotion to

Shakspeare, if too exclusive, recommends him to our national pride. He has published a Trilogy of tales on the life of Shakspeare, full of poetry, thought, and exquisite appretiation of his hero, and of the cotemporary poets, which I mean, some time or other, to translate, if it does not fall into abler hands.

I subjoin some remarks by the same hand to which I am indebted for those on Friedrich von Schlegel.

" If we venture to add anything to the short biographical notice of this extraordinary man, we must entreat our readers to bear in mind the contents of the note on Friedrich von Schlegel. We must try, above all, to conceive of German literature, as of a great living Whole. For in no country have men of genius acted upon and through each other so powerfully as in Germany ;—in none have they so laboured, hand in hand, at the universal advancement and culture. Read but the correspondence of Schiller and Goethe. How does every line bespeak that they regarded it as their highest and holiest task to educate the nation,— to refine its taste, and enlarge its intelligence.

" Novalis, too, regarded this as the true vocation of every poet ; and this is the real reason why he plunged so deep into abstract reasonings—this is the reason why German writers generally devote themselves to criticism and æsthetics to a degree we find in no other nation. Each poet of England appears rather in the light of an isolated individual; and, with the exception, perhaps, of Pope and his cotemporaries, none of them form what can be properly called *a school*—a band of writers united to work in one direction, and to one end*.

"Novalis, although a friend of the Schlegels, and forming a school with them, Tieck, and some others of less note, stood infinitely higher as *man*. His personal friendship was, therefore, devoted to a soul as pure and elevated as his own. This he found in the noble-minded Friedrich Heinrich Jacobi, who has acquired so high a reputation in the *history* of philosophy.

"Their characters were, in some respects, similar. We shall give some account of the philosophical opinions which they held in common, and which were essentially incorporated in Novalis's poetry, when we come to speak more particularly of Ja-

* It seems to me that this description applies eminently to the French poets of the 18th century. The poets composing our 'Lake school' seem hardly to have warked with sufficient unity and definiteness of aim.— *Transl.*

cobi. Suffice it to say here, that the profounder tendency given to philosophy by Jacobi and Schelling, and which may be ultimately traced up to Spinoza, was in direct and avowed hostility to the reigning school,—to those half lights which had been in fashion ; and, as the best heads were numbered among its followers, the victory must infallibly have been theirs, had they not plunged, *par contrecoup*, into the opposite extreme—into a sort of philosophico-religious mysticism.

" We must acknowledge with regret, that together with beauties and excellencies of the highest order, there is, in Novalis's works, much of this play of the imagination with whatever is picturesque and sentimental in the Christian religion, and that the element of the Wonderful, the Wild, and the Fantastic is much too predominant. This is felt by every reader of his *Heinrich von Ofterdingen.*

" Heinrich was a Minnesänger, and one of the competitors for the prize at the celebrated contest on the Wartburg. Novalis chose him for his hero, as affording an opportunity of describing, in the form of a biographical romance, the growth and development of a poetical mind. The work, however, never proceeded beyond the second volume, and is unfinished. It begins with the moment at which

Heinrich quits the paternal house, and sets out on his way to Augsburg, then the centre of German opulence and civilization, in company with several merchants of substance and education. Before he reaches the city, various adventures befal him; among others, he wanders into a cave where he finds a wonderful old man, who shows him his future destiny, in a book consisting of mysterious symbolical pictures. His aspirations now become clearer and more intelligible to his own mind; his intense love for legends, his fantasies, his dreams of the blue wonderflower (*Wunderblume*) which is the object of his ceaseless and ardent longings— all tell him that he is called to be a poet.

" Arrived in Augsburg, he is received into the splendid house of the magnificent Klingshorn, who then held sway as prince of German poets. At first the young Heinrich is enchanted by the gaiety, the pomp, and the festive splendours of the stately city; the attractive and elegant tone of society, the sports and dances; he cannot fail to admire the poetical fertility, the lightness, ease, and grace peculiar to the matured Klingshorn; yet, after a while, he feels himself a stranger and an alien in the world of pleasure. He feels that this is no place for the study of life, or for the nurture of poetry. The talents and the universality of Klingshorn appear

P

to him too earthly, and their direction too little serious. Poetry has, to his feelings, a higher, and a holier vocation. Even the captivating Mathilde, the daughter of his host, has no power to enchain him, He leaves the city, resumes his wanderings in his own visionary world, and arrives at the grand meeting on the Wartburg, where he hears the greatest poets of the time, Wolfram von Eschilbach, Walter von der Vogelweide, and Klingshorn himself, contend for the laurel. Heinrich is permitted to give some proof of his own poetical powers, which as yet do not burst forth with victorious splendour, but rather, in a sort of warning prelude, give note of the fire and the force that lie hidden within him.

" It is not the object of this short notice to go into the details of the work. We call the attention of our readers only to what immediately conduces to our aim—the elucidation of the relation in which the youthful Heinrich von Ofterdingen stood to Klingshorn. In the contrast he draws between the matured man of the world and sovereign poet, and the dreaming youth whose merits and whose success are of a far less dazzling character, Novalis evidently represents that between himself and Goethe, whose portrait in Klingshorn is not to be mistaken. In fragments which appeared at a later period, he expressed himself more plainly and decidedly concerning Goethe, and especially in opposition to the tendency of *Wilhelm Meister* *.

" In order to give a just conception of this opposition, we must slightly touch upon some of the most important circumstances of that period of literature. Goethe's *Wilhelm Meister* gave rise to a new didactic kind of novel, which, under the name of *Kunst*, or *Künstler Romane* (Novels of Art, or Artist-Novels), has been a very prevailing

---

* I find among the scraps from which those alluded to above were selected, the following. I remember suppressing it, because I thought it not fair to Goethe to give it without explanation ; and because I did not agree with the author. It will be seen that the author uses the word *atheism* in a different and much wider sense than it bears among us.

" Wilhelm Meister's Apprenticeship is, in a certain sense, thoroughly prosaic and modern. The Romantic is completely levelled in it—so is the poetry of nature, the Wonderful. The book treats only of the ordinary affairs of men ; Nature and the Mysterious (*Mysticismus*) are utterly forgotten. It is a poeticized, civic and domestic story; the Wonderful in it is expressly treated as fiction and enthusiastic dreaming (*Schwärmerei*). Artist-like Atheism is the spirit of the book. The economy is worthy of note, with which it produces a poetical effect, by means of cheap, prosaic stuff."—*Transl.*

sort of reading in Germany up to the present time. The author takes either a fictitious or a historical personage; and, in the narrative of his life, gradually, and in accordance with his own views and maxims, developes the progress of the peculiar art to which his hero has devoted himself. We shall mention only the most remarkable of these works. Goethe's *Wilhelm Meister* is justly considered as reaching beyond the sphere of these mere imaginary portraits of the life and genius of an artist. It was by no means the design of the great poet, (as was long erroneously imagined,) to pourtray the progress of a young man in the dramatic art. The mistake of the public was, however, pardonable, since a large portion of the book relates to the drama; but in the last volume, the author dismisses that topic, and here the grand aim of the book comes to light. Goethe meant to describe the *general* growth and ripening of a youth of talent into *Man*. His passion for the drama is only a transition state, and brings him no permanent satisfaction. His education for Life, for free and active exertion in a higher field, is the true end.

"The school of Tieck and Novalis were displeased with this. They thought that the poet who had given hints and glimpses of such grandeur of conception ought to have ended his work in something more than the education of an accomplished man of the world. The object seemed to them too earthly; and Novalis, who was far too fastidious, reserved, and high-minded a person to engage in a paper war, expressed his disapprobation of the tendency of the book (both as a matter of philosophical speculation and of religious feeling) only in short but significant hints.

" His *Heinrich von Ofterdingen* is, in every line, a mirror of his own child-like character. But his pure, beautiful, and enthusiastic nature, however noble and engaging it may appear, belonged too little to this world, and was not qualified to grasp the manysided, giant mind of Goethe.

" Tieck selected for the subject of his *Kunstroman* the education of a painter. Franz Sternbald is a young German painter, who grows up under the pure influence of German art—of the works of Albrecht Dürer, Lucas Kranach, &c. He then goes to Italy, where he admires the richer and more gorgeous creations of the *aureo secolo*, and revels, for a while, in an Italian atmosphere of warmth and beauty. This novel, like *Heinrich von Ofterdingen*, is unfinished. Tieck breaks off the thread of the story in Italy; but the reader is led to conjecture that Franz Sternbald, sated with the luxuriant beauty of the south, will return to the bosom of German simplicity, and recognize the cultivation of the severer graces as the true, holy vocation of Art.

" The *Kunstroman* assumed another form after the appearance of Goethe's *Tasso*, and a host of imitators wrote *Künstlerdramen* (lives of artists in a dramatic form). Among the most celebrated are Öhlenschläger's *Coreggio** and Immerman's *Petrarca*. The other numerous attempts are scarcely worthy of notice.

" We may be permitted to add two extracts, which characterize Novalis's turn of mind, and show that Art was, with him, an object of holy earnestness.

" ' In youth we read history from curiosity alone, as we would an amusing story. In riper age we regard her as a heavenly, consoling, and instructive friend, who softly prepares our way to a higher and more extensive career by her wise converse, and makes us acquainted with the unknown world by means of intelligible symbols. The Church is

---

* An account of the delicate and touching beauties of this tragedy, accompanied with excellent translations, appeared in Blackwood's Magazine, which has contained so many admirable articles on German literature. I think, but am not certain, that the whole was not translated.—*Transl.*

the dwelling-house of history' (here Novalis's religious feelings break out), 'and the quiet churchyard her symbolical flower-garden. History should be written only by old and god-fearing men, whose own history is at an end, and who have nothing further to hope than their transplantation into that garden. And their description would not be dark or gloomy; much rather would *a ray from the cupola* show every thing in the most just and beautiful light, and the Holy Spirit would move upon the face of these strangely troubled waters.'"

" ' Poetry must, especially, be pursued as a *severe* art. As mere pleasure—amusement—it ceases to be poetry. A poet must not wander about idly all day long, hunting for images and for sensations. That is the wholly perverted way. A pure open spirit, a habit of reflection and of observation, and skill in putting all his powers into a reciprocally quickening activity, and in holding them therein,— such are the qualities demanded of a poet.' "—

(*Ad. H.*)

Note 19.

Goethe here alludes to Ernst Schulze (b. 1789), author of the *Cecilie*, the *Bezauberte Rose* (Enchanted Rose), and other poems, the former of which was conceived in the first agony of his grief at the loss of the beautiful and amiable girl of that name, to whom he was entirely devoted. She died in 1813, at the age of eighteen. The feeling of his loss seems never to have abandoned him for an instant; every thing he did had reference to her, and even his patriotic enthusiasm was mingled with devotion to her memory. An account of Schulze's character and poems appeared in the Foreign Quarterly Review,—as also one chiefly taken from it, with due acknowledgement, in Mr. Taylor's third volume. Schulze took arms as a volunteer, in 1814. I cannot resist the temptation to copy, from the article in question, the following beautiful translation of a little poem of his, written on that occasion, which compelled him to suspend the labours he had consecrated to the memory of Cecilia:

> " Steeds are neighing, swords are gleaming,
>   Germany's revenge is nigh,
> And the banners brightly gleaming,
>   Wave us on to victory.

Rouse thee, then, fond heart, and see
For a time thy task forsaken;
Bear what life hath laid on thee,
And forget what it hath taken."

Goethe's mention of this unfortunate young poet may appear hard and unfeeling. But it ought to be borne in mind, that Goethe strongly disapproved and systematically discouraged, this abandonment of the mind to one set of impressions—this entire loss of the equipoise (*Gleichgewicht*), of which we constantly find him speaking with admiration and reverence, as the consummation of the character of Man, and which it was the effort of his whole life to acquire and to maintain. He had passed through the Wertherian and many other states, and no one regarded that condition of the human mind with less respect. He, too, who was the most objective of poets (except, perhaps, Shakspeare), might be expected to view with some impatience the intensely subjective scheme of Schulze's poems.

Schulze died of consumption, in 1817. His works have had no permanent influence on German literature.

NOTE 20.

I have received from Germany a little memoir of this admirable woman, and one of her husband, Duke Karl August, by Chancellor von Müller, of Weimar, for whose memoir of Goethe (*Goethe in seiner praktische Wirksamkeit*) I am indebted to the kindness of Frau von Goethe. I thought them too long and too considerable for notes, and have subjoined them in the third volume.

NOTE 21.

Duke Karl Wilhelm Ferdinand of Braunschweig, born in 1735, eldest son of the reigning Duke Karl, and of a sister of Frederic the Great. He early displayed a thirst for glory, which the example of his uncle served to render more intense. The seven years' war afforded him the first opportunity of distinguishing himself, and justified the expression of Frederic, " that Nature had formed him for a hero." He married the Princess Au-

gusta of Wales. As he had early learned the condition of his country, and the continual embar-
rassments of his father had read him an useful
lesson, he laid down to himself rules of the severest
economy, and lived retired from public affairs and
devoted chiefly to art and science. He succeeded
his father in 1780, and entered on the duties of
his office with earnestness and activity. He diminished the expenses of the court, discharged a
part of the public debt, and attempted many things
for the education and advantage of his people—not
always with the best-success. In 1787, he took
the command of a Prussian army destined to re-
instate the Stadtholder of Holland. This cam-
paign was so quickly and easily terminated, that
it gained him, perhaps, more fame than it deserved, and led to exaggerated expectations of his
success in the disastrous enterprize against the
armies of the French revolution. He was appointed
commander of the Austrian and Prussian troops;
and, in 1792, published that celebrated manifesto
which had been drawn up in very violent language
by a Frenchman named De Limon. The Emperor
Francis and the King of Prussia approved it, but
the Duke thought the expressions too strong. The
bitterest were struck out; the Prussian General,
Legationsrath von Renfner, arranged the whole,

and the Prussian envoy at Mainz, Herr von Stein, had it printed. The consequences are well known.

In 1794, he resigned his command, and from that time till 1806, devoted himself entirely to the improvement of his country. His edict concerning schools, bearing that date, is a model for all rulers. At an advanced age, when he might without reproach have withdrawn from the toils of war, he undertook burthens which surpassed his strength. He once more took the command of the Prussian army. The disparity between his moral and physical powers was fatally proved at the battle of Jena and Auerstadt.

Mortally wounded, he was obliged to quit his paternal soil, and breathed his last at Ottensen, near Altona, November, 1808. This unfortunate prince undoubtedly misunderstood his own powers. He lived in times long gone by.

But his character as a ruler is without reproach; his greatest enemies cannot deny that his government was most beneficent. The want of unity of will, which showed itself in many of the acts of his life, was probably the cause of the failure of some of his benevolent designs. His subjects reproached him with partiality for the French, which he had contracted from his uncle, and which he bitterly expiated.—(*Abridged from the Convers.-Lex.*)

NOTE 22.

Lucas Kranach's real name was Sünder. Like many of the Italian artists, he took the name of his birthplace, Kranach, or Kronach, in the bishopric of Bamberg. He was born in 1472, one year after the birth of Albrecht Dürer.

His father was a model-maker and illuminator; from him he learnt some of the mechanical part of his art. He early went to Koburg, where Friedrich the Wise, Elector of Saxony, founder of the university of Wittenberg, discovered his talents and took him home to his court. He accompanied him on his journey to the Holy Land in 1493, and from that time began his career as historical painter. In 1504, he was appointed court-painter to the elector and to his brother, Duke Johann Friedrich, and was ennobled by them. In 1537 he was chosen Bürgermeister of Wittenberg. Johann Friedrich, who had succeeded to the electorate, and had joined the alliance of Protestant prin-ces against the Emperor Charles V., was taken prisoner at the battle of Mühlberg. Charles treated him with great severity, and delivered him over to a military tribunal composed of Italians and Spaniards, with Alba at their head. He was condemned to death, and only preserved his life by the renunciation of his electoral dignity and hereditary estates. In spite of these concessions, he was thrown into prison at Innspruck. At the siege of Wittenberg, which took place shortly after the battle of Mühlberg, Charles is reported to have testified his admiration for the genius and works of Lucas Kranach, and to have promised him any favour he might ask. Kranach fell on his knees and besought him to liberate his captive master. This was, however, more than the emperor thought fit to grant, and the faithful painter then entreated to be allowed to share his captivity, which he did till its termination. At the capitulation of Wittenberg, after five years of imprisonment, Johann Friedrich was allowed to return to Saxony, but with the loss of his electoral dignity and the greater part of his dominions, which Prince Moritz, the illustrious champion of Protestantism, had transferred to the Albertinian line of Saxony. The Ernestinian line retained little but the Thuringian part of its possessions. Of this, Weimar was the capital, and became in consequence the residence of the duke. The houses of Sachsen-Weimar, Gotha, Meiningen-Hilburghausen, Altenburg, and Koburg-Gotha are all branches of the Ernestinian line. Johann Friedrich died within two years from his liberation, and his faithful follower one year after.

He lies buried in the church belonging to the palace at Weimar. The curious blunder of the stone engraver, who has inscribed his tomb *Pictor celerrimus*, instead of *celeberrimus*, is almost justified by the number of his works scattered over the galleries and collections of Germany. Some of these, however, may probably be more justly ascribed to his son, who bore the same name, and was a worthy pupil of his father. The works of Kranach are distinguished by accurate drawing, truth of expression, fidelity to nature, delicacy of touch, and by extraordinary brilliancy and beauty of colouring, which three centuries have not impaired. Lucas, like his great cotemporary Albrecht Dürer, had the truth, vigour, and deep feeling of nature which characterize genius.

The most valuable of his portraits are those of his friends Luther and Melancthon, whose faith he, as well as his unfortunate master, had adopted. There is a celebrated altar-piece by bim, in a church at Weimar, and also at Wittenberg. The former was restored by Meyer, in 1806. A work, *Über den Leben und die Werke Lucas Kranachs*, was published at Bamberg in 1821.

There is a collection of miniature portraits,

painted in water colours on parchment, which the painter called his album (*Stammbuch*). In 1797 Chancellor and Prince von Hardenberg bought this interesting book out of the collection of Hofrath Lämmermann, of Anspach, and presented it to King Freidrich Wilhelm II. The gift reached him in his last illness, and was neglected and forgotten. It was not till 1812 that it was found and brought into notice, at Berlin, by Herr von Mechel. The heads have a singular air of life; they are as follows :—1. Our Saviour.—2. Friedrich III. surnamed the Wise, Elector of Saxony.—3. His successor, Johann Friedrich, surnamed the Magnanimous.—4. Johann Ernst, Duke of Koburg.—5. Martin Luther.—6. Philip Melancthon.—7. Justus Jonas.—8. Johann Bugenhagen.—9. George Spalatin.—10. Lucas Kranach himself, as he appears in the altar-piece at Weimar, standing beneath the Cross of Christ. Short notices of these personages, so celebrated in the history of the Reformation, and autographs of the four Doctors of Theology, are annexed.—(*Abridged from the Conversations-Lexicon.*)

This *Stammbuch* was published at Berlin in 1814. A copy of it is in the possession of a friend of mine in this country.

Addenda to Note 2.

There is an interesting little biographical memoir of Gore inserted in Goethe's life of Philip Hackert, the artist, with whom Gore lived in great intimacy at Rome. It concludes in these words :

" The presence of this excellent man is to be remembered among the greatest advantages this town (Weimar) has, of late years, enjoyed. His personal qualities had a uniformly beneficent influence. He was simple, friendly, and obliging to every one; even at an advanced age, his countenance and person made a most agreeable impression. His fortune enabled him to surround himself with comforts and conveniences, and to show himself liberal to all,—to give encouragement to industry and talent, and succour to distress. The perfect uniformity of his behaviour rendered his society equable and agreeable ; and even when he was suffering from gout, he was cheerful, sympathising, and amusing."

He died at Weimar, and is buried there, with two of his daughters. His youngest daughter married Lord Cowper, at Florence. The whole family were great favourites with the court of Weimar.

———

The following curious description of a fancy of Goethe's has been kindly given me by a friend :

" In 1810, I saw, in the hands of my friend Aldebert, at Frankfurt, a caricature in water colours, executed by Mrs. A's uncle, Kraus of Weimar ; but I learned from Herr von Knebel, afterwards, that the caricature was the invention of Goethe himself. It included a number of figures, of which I retain but a very imperfect recollection. One group consisted of a procession of young men, following a hearse, each with a pistol at his head. No explanation of this is necessary. Another procession is formed of two youths, in old German costume, on two prancing steeds ; in front real horses, but the rear cast into shadow, being a long board. The heroes, in fact, were riding, like children, a cock-horse. These, I was told, were the two Counts Stolberg, who, in their youth, were famed as patriotic poets. One afterwards acquired a sad celebrity, by turning catholic. A third group was an owl perched on a German oak, below which was a duck, greedily swallowing what fell. I understood this to allude to a book written by Ebers, in idolatrous praise of Klopstock, with the fantastic title of *Er, und über ihn* (He, and about him); and I have some faint impression that these little words were traced on the ground by what the duck was devouring with such alacrity."

H. C. R.

END OF VOL. I.

Arthur Taylor, Printer, 39, Coleman street.

Lightning Source UK Ltd.
Milton Keynes UK
UKHW021147080119
335202UK00012B/543/P